# Minor Theater
## Three Plays

53SP 25
March 2017

ISBN 978-0-9897393-6-8
Library of Congress Control No. 2017936499

53rdstatepress.org
© Julia Jarcho 2017

Front cover: Jenny Seastone in *Grimly Handsome*. Photo by Alex Fabozzi.
Back cover: Jenny Seastone and Ben Williams in *Dreamless Land*. Photo courtesy
New York City Players.

# Minor Theater
# Three Plays

Julia Jarcho

*53rd State Press*
*Brooklyn, New York*
*2017*

To be as a stranger *in* one's own language.

—Deleuze and Guattari, "What Is a Minor Literature?"

I might be an adult, but I'm a minor at heart.

—Minor Threat, "Minor Threat"

*For Jane*

# Contents

# Interview

TIM REID: There's something about the speed with which your writing moves…

JULIA JARCHO: A lot of the pleasure of the theater for me is something like the pleasure of a private joke. Not because the content is "sophisticated" or whatever, but because the whole event is contingent: something happens to be funny to this handful of people right now. At my shows, what I really want is for people to be laughing throughout the play but at unpredictable moments, at different moments. I don't need people to be laughing together. It's something about experiencing pleasure as not guaranteeable, not stable. Something exciting about that.

TR: Your writing is so prose-aware. I'm aware of it as writing at the same time I'm aware of it as part of the play.

JJ: I think when you experience language as writing, you experience distance, which is space—room for something new to develop. I tend to feel better about working with actors who can maintain a certain degree of distance in their performance. Not like total coldness, but some margin. I was talking about this with Ben Williams, an actor I work with a lot, and he said when he's looking at a script he's thinking not "Why would this character say this?" but "Why would this writer write this?" Not what is the character thinking, but what is the writer thinking. And I think that's a good match for my plays.

At the same time I do think an excitement about spoken language is a big part of how I write. But that includes a lot of different situations of spoken language, and often ones that are already formalized, like genre writing. Film noir dialogue, for example, you learn that style by hearing it first, by watching and listening to people in movies. So even though it's impossible that anyone could ever speak that way "naturally," it still is an oral structure. I'm always writing through sound, working out the words as a certain pattern of sounds.

TR: How do you keep characters distinct as identities disintegrate? That's part of the fun, part of the play. Becoming indistinct, but maintaining a clarity through that.

JJ: My good friend and collaborator Ásta Bennie Hostetter, a costume designer, brought this up recently. We were trying to think through what is fundamental to the work we do as a company, and she mentioned this thing about metamorphosis, and the instability of identity. For one thing the actors tend to play multiple characters. But then there's also a certain amount of ambiguity about what a "character" is—that's also always shifting, subject to change. That's fun for me, watching performers create that. Jenny Seastone is masterful at it. Of course you can talk about it ethically too. The lie we tell by pretending that people are coherent wholes—that's irresponsible, besides being depressing and boring.

And I'm also not that interested in replicating the big emotions that are easy to recognize from "real life." Don't we have enough of those? So for instance, my father died when I was 23, that's not so remarkable, but I know a lot of what I write is still responding to that loss. And I could try to express it directly in a way that would invite audiences to see their own losses in mine. But there are already so many structures in place to support that kind of experience by selling it back to you—on every channel, on every bookshelf. I'm more interested in building structures for kinds of experience that aren't legitimated by various discourses of suffering and healing, and don't need to be. Surprising, weird, interstitial feelings and fantasies. Not the stuff that makes us who we are, but the stuff that interrupts us.

*Tim Reid is a writer and performer living in Los Angeles. He has been conducting research for a project on clown.*

# Grimly Handsome

*a play in three parts*

*Grimly Handsome* premiered in New York City at Incubator Arts Project's Other Forces festival in January 2013. It was directed by the author and performed by Jenny Seastone, Pete Simpson, and Ben Williams. Sets were designed by Jason Simms, costumes by Ásta Bennie Hostetter, sound by Cooper Gardner, and lights by Barbara Samuels. Henry Cheng was the assistant director and stage manager, Katie Ferrari was the assistant stage manager, and Jess Chayes was the producer.

*Characters*

Alesh/Alpert/Alfo

Gregor/Greggins/Grox

Natalia/Nelly/Nally/Noplop


*Place*

New York City


*Time*

Recently


*Notes*

In Part One, Alesh and Gregor are talking to each other in their native language (even though what we hear is English), so there are no accents. When they address other people, they switch to English, in which they have Slavic or Balkan accents.

A slash / in a line indicates that the following line starts at this point and overlaps with this one.

Line breaks might indicate either a rhythmic break or something like a cut between two takes of a film. They might also indicate that a song or a poem is being performed.

# Part One. The Low

*Outside a trailer where Gregor and Alesh are living while they sell Christmas trees. The trees around them. Also, Natalia's room.*

## Scene 1

*Nighttime. Alesh and Gregor are sitting outside. Light from a police car flickers off their faces, then passes by. A siren once, slow.*

ALESH: I wanted that.

> *Pause.*

> To be in the police.

GREGOR: English.

ALESH: Uck. Later.

> *Pause.*

GREGOR: What police?

ALESH: Oh

> In the village.

GREGOR: I never was in your village. What was it called?

> *Pause.*

> You have to be crazy for power.

ALESH: Yes, well, I like it.

GREGOR: Not enough.

ALESH: Yes.

GREGOR: In my city, the police were friendly with the dogs.

ALESH: Not the——

GREGOR: Yes, the wild packs. The commander would stand in the middle of the square and whistle through his fingers. Everyone else would run, duck into shops. And the dogs would appear. They came right up to him. And he gave them gifts.

ALESH: He fed them.

GREGOR: No. He gave them other things.

*Pause.*

ALESH: I had a dog.

GREGOR: While the dogs were there his men would shoot them. Just some of them. The others wouldn't notice or

Didn't bother them.

ALESH: His name was Alesh.

GREGOR: They still would come.

ALESH: My name.

GREGOR: You'll see.

ALESH: Mm.

GREGOR: You'll see.

*The siren sounds again. Gregor and Alesh sit and watch.*

## Scene 2

*Daytime. Alesh and Gregor are drinking coffee from mugs. There is a customer.*

GREGOR: This one, ninety-five. Special price.

ALESH: No problem, we are here.

*The customer leaves.*

So?

GREGOR: So. About seven o'clock p.m. I see her down the block, towards the train, she's coming from work. There are other people on the street, but

15

not so many, it's as dark as it will be for the night. But I can see that it's her because, because of the street light. And she comes smiling and

goes by.

Hey!

She stops.

She comes back.

Hello.

How you doing.

She says Ok, how bout you?

I say shrug.

Trees selling like hotcakes?

Yes, like hot cakes.

Coming from work?

She says Yeah well. She says she took a detour. She has a look of mystery. I say: Christmas shopping? She laughs. And she says "sure."

Now: I have to be careful. I say, would you like to take another detour? But I don't point to the trailer or anything, I'm careful. I make a joke, I say, walk in the forest? Here wait, just wait one minute. And she waits. And I bring her:

*Alesh looks down at his coffee. He takes a sip.*

ALESH: Yeah?

GREGOR: Beer, no, it can make them uncomfortable. Tea, makes you seem old. She takes it:

*Gregor drinks.*

And she says, Now I'll never get to sleep tonight.

I say: Maybe not.

ALESH: Gregor!

GREGOR: What?

ALESH: Why tell me this?

GREGOR: You're bored?

ALESH: It has nothing to do with me.

GREGOR: It's a good story.

ALESH: Not really.

GREGOR: It's instructive.

ALESH: Not for me.

GREGOR: Oh?

ALESH: I like to help people. I like to make them happy. I don't even like to think about myself and my desires. That's even a big problem for me. I need to work on that. What you're talking about, it's not the kind of person I am.

*Beat. Alesh laughs long and hard.*

I'm gonna go get a cruller.

Fuck it.

Want?

*Alesh exits. Natalia enters. She looks at the trees. Gregor watches her.*

NATALIA: How much is this one?

GREGOR: One-fifty.

NATALIA: One hundred fifty?

GREGOR: We have all different size.

*Natalia looks at some more trees.*

NATALIA: How bout this one?

GREGOR: This one?

You don't like.

NATALIA: Why? How much?

GREGOR: Also one-fifty.

NATALIA: But it's so much shorter.

GREGOR: Douglas Fir.

NATALIA: Ohhh.

GREGOR: Oprah, she has.

NATALIA: Oprah?

GREGOR: How much you will spend?

NATALIA: I thought. Thirty?

*Gregor goes off, returns with a tiny tree.*

GREGOR: This one: twenty-five.

NATALIA: Mm ok, that's ok. Thank you. Good night.

*She starts to exit.*

GREGOR: You TAKE.

NATALIA: What?

GREGOR: You, you take. No one wants. Present. You want bigger, you can come back, pay.

NATALIA: W…

GREGOR: TAKE

NATALIA: Thanks. That's very nice.

*She picks up the tree.*

How do I keep it fresh?

GREGOR: It's dead.

*Natalia leaves with the little tree.*

*Silence for a while as Gregor guards the trees. Then he picks up a radio and turns it on. Christmas music plays. He sets the radio down. Alesh returns, holding a paper bag.*

ALESH: I got you one.

*Gregor declines. Alesh eats the cruller. He notices the music.*

What's that.

GREGOR: To drum up trade.

ALESH: It's awful.

*Music plays. Alesh sits.*

It's AWFUL.

*Alesh moves toward the radio. Gregor stops him with a look. Alesh fumes. Alesh goes inside the trailer. Sound of rummaging. Gregor listens, alert. Alesh comes out wearing big feminine earmuffs.*

GREGOR: Take that off.

*Alesh doesn't hear, or pretends not to hear.*

Take it

*Alesh lifts off one earmuff.*

ALESH: Hmm?

GREGOR: That's mine.

ALESH: I never saw you wear it.

*Tense pause. Alesh takes off the earmuffs and hands them to Gregor. Gregor takes them inside the trailer. Alesh turns off the radio. Gregor comes out. They look at each other.*

No one enjoys to hear that shit. They run away in horror.

GREGOR: No, that's our perspective.

If you have no culture, that's your culture.

*Alesh hands Gregor the radio.*

ALESH: Fuck it, was free from the bank.

GREGOR: What bank.

ALESH: No, there was a table outside, a promotion. She said I could take. Even without opening an account. Because I'm handsome.

GREGOR: Who said.

ALESH: Whoever.

GREGOR: Said that?

ALESH: That was the reason anyway.

*Gregor hands the radio back to him.*

GREGOR: You took it from her. It's yours.

*Alesh sits down. Gregor regards him.*

I don't find you handsome.

ALESH: You're blind.

# Scene 3

*Natalia in her apartment. The little tree is there, unattended to. Natalia reads from a paperback. She keeps her scarf on.*

NATALIA: Dominic dropped the butt of his cigarette and crushed it under the sole of his Hugo Boss loafer. He had always taken a lot of shit from the guys over what they called his "fancy" way of dressing, but he'd never even been tempted to give it up. He was a firm believer that most people treated you better, took you more seriously, once you gave them a look at your market value. "Lawrence is an asshole," he said simply.

Moran shrugged. "Nothing I can do about that. But Dom, he wants you on this too. He may be an asshole but he knows an ace profiler when he sees one. And you're the best in the business."

Dominic hated flattery worse than low-sodium soup, but he could tell Moran was being sincere. "All right," he said. "Have the boys messenger me the crime scene photos ASAP. And tell the asshole I'll take the case."

It was to be the most fateful decision of his life.

## Scene 4

*Alesh and Gregor are training.*

ALESH: Um. Excuse me. What is your name.

GREGOR: That's what the rats say to her. She won't stop.

ALESH: Natalia!

GREGOR: Not her name.

ALESH: Could be.

GREGOR: The odds are terrible.

ALESH: Like this: Natalia! Oh I'm sorry. Wait. I'm sorry, but, you look so much like my cousin Natalia. And I haven't seen her in a long time. You're not from the village? Our village, no, American. Well it's a nice compliment, Natalia is very beautiful, everyone agrees. Hey. Would you like a cup of coffee? I just made some. You can smell it, it's good. From back home.

GREGOR: Ha!

ALESH: Oh good! let me get you a, please.

*Gregor sits.*

Uh, it's my first time this year. The guy I work with, he's been doing it a long time. You've seen him probably yeah, kind of a freak of a fellow. But he has a good heart.

But what about you?

GREGOR: English.

ALESH: (Ungrh.) Next time in English?

But what about you?

GREGOR: "Me, oh. Hardship. Decisions."

ALESH: Huh, wow.

GREGOR: "Someone might rape me, I have high co-pays."

ALESH: Yeah tell me about it.

GREGOR: "I used to think of myself as an artist. I can't read the news, it's too depressing."

ALESH: You're right.

GREGOR: Too soft.

ALESH: But no I think: no, it's important to read the news. This is a democracy, if the people don't read the news, how can you govern?

GREGOR: "But I'm afraid of what I'm going to read."

ALESH: Don't be afraid.

You're safe.

GREGOR: Fast Forward.

*Gregors goes floppy in his chair.*

ALESH: Are you all right?

GREGOR: I'm. Is. Shit. Help!

ALESH: You don't feel well? Want me to call someone?

GREGOR: But. Help!

ALESH: What can I do? What's wrong?

GREGOR: English.

ALESH: What —what—What's wrong?— What can I do?— What—

GREGOR: Or:

*They switch places. Gregor holds Alesh.*

You're a mouse in my hand.

You're safe.

The dip behind your head where my finger rests

and the shine of the fur

Don't move

time is stopping

Don't move

time is stopped

*Pause.*

TAKE

ALESH: TAKE

*Gregor exits.*

Come on Natalia, let's lie you down where it's warm.

## Scene 5

*Natalia's apartment. Natalia reads.*

NATALIA: The cook was completely bald, with beady eyes, and sweating profusely. "Help you?" "I wonder if you can," said Dominic. "I'm looking for someone I hear's a regular customer of yours." "Look around," said the man, and started shuffling back in the direction of the kitchen. "Hang on." The cook turned around. He was a good head taller than Dominic, and now he fastened on the detective's blue eyes with his own beady ones. "You police?" Dominic—

*Natalia is no longer reading.*

Dominic. Says the cook. Let me tell you about it. Let me explain what you are seeing. This is a moment of great global unhappiness. What are the clues. Come on. A rat. Yes: a little animal rife with disease. Making its nest in your shoe. The bodies of lesser creatures lying all over the room. Plundered. Chyewed. Now. Do you make friends or what.

Dominic says: I don't go in for parables.

The cook says: It's very simple. There's always someone waiting.

# Scene 6

*Morning light rises on Alesh outside the trailer. He gets a spray bottle, sprays the trees. He sings to himself softly.*

ALESH: My only one
    it is
    mm hmm hmm
    you are
    mm hmm hmm
    no business
    of them…

*Customer.*

    Ninety-five. Beautiful tree. Very fresh. Keep till New Year.
    Yeah? Ok sir. One minute, I wrap.
    This way.

*Alesh carries the tree around back. Beat. Gregor emerges from the trailer with the spray bottle. He continues the song as he goes to spray the trees.*

GREGOR: When I come
    it is
    mm hmm hmm
    you are
    mm hmm hmm
    you are my…

*Gregor sees that the trees are recently sprayed. Nods and smiles at someone walking past.*

    Jessica
    Sylvia
    Sylvia

Dear mothers and fathers, I say, don't name them. It's asking for help. The kind you don't want.

Kate

It's the sense of being someone that gets them.

Pennsylvania

I call you by the wrong name and it's an act of protest. My mind is sharp like a pick. It's an act of action. To say: fuck your enthusiasm.

*Pause.*

I'm going to see you in this dark place, maybe it's a Night Club.
Or it's a wide street in an industrial district.

No trash, no commerce. Why would you come to this place?

You left your home, your sleeping ones, their bodies warming and smells, their undefended faces.

You tucked them in tighter and you shut their bedroom doors. If they had woken up they would have wondered why you have your coat on. Plus it's your coat for when you want to impress. You're wearing your formal coat.

Let me tell you, your formal coat is a disgrace. Everything you put on yourself is shabby. Everything that touches you gives up right away. There is a myasma

that gets out ahead of you, behind you, no matter how much you deplore it

and succeeds in spoiling more than you could know

as you know

's enough. I came here to let you know that it's worse than you feared.

To help you to fear, to cover yourself in your fear, since even your coat falls off of you in shreds.

*Natalia enters. Gregor sees her without looking at her.*

Yeah. So there is a vacant lot with a high wire fence all around.

NATALIA: Oh, I. Have one. A small one.

    *She looks up at the big tree. Looks back at Alesh.*

    You

    *Pause.*

ALESH: Hm?
NATALIA: Thanks.

    *Natalia exits.*

GREGOR: She likes you.
ALESH: She's weird.

# Scene 7

*Natalia is going to deal with the little tree. She tries setting it in various locations. Finally she places it right in front of her chair and sits staring at it. She stands up. She sits down. She stands up again. She cases the tree. She takes out a lighter. She considers setting the tree on fire. She crouches by the tree. She almost lights it. But she doesn't. She apologizes to the tree.*

NATALIA: Sorry.
    I'm sorry.

    *She goes back to her chair and sits looking at the tree.*

# Scene 8

*Alesh and Gregor in front of the trailer.*

ALESH: There was an old woman in the village. When we were little. She was this, like, repulsive person. She would spit giant—

> *Gregor holds up his hand.*

> Yeah. So, but. One day we were trying to look in her window and she caught us and made us come inside and fed us cake. Her house had a smell.

GREGOR: Bad?

ALESH: No. Like a certain kind of spice or herb? I don't know maybe a flower, dried flower.

> She used to suck me off.

> Then give me cake.

> And one time stew. With big pieces of

> soldiers

GREGOR: Natalia.

ALESH: Who?

> *Beat.*

> Ah. Yeah?

GREGOR: She's yours.

ALESH: Yeah.

GREGOR: I won't interfere.

ALESH: Good.

GREGOR: I'll be invisible.

> *Gregor exits.*

## Scene 9

*Alesh in front of the trailer. Natalia walks by. She stops. She looks at the trees. She looks at Alesh furtively, then back at the trees.*

ALESH: Hi.
NATALIA: Hi.
ALESH: You woulding for ssthnthing?

> *Beat.*

NATALIA: What?
ALESH: Ha. I'm.
> Who are you. —How are you.
NATALIA: Good.

> *Beat.*

> How are you?
ALESH: I'm good.

> *Natalia nods, smiles.*

> I know your name.
NATALIA: You do?
ALESH: Yeah.

> *Beat.*

NATALIA: What is it?
ALESH: Guess.

> *Beat.*

NATALIA: I give up.
ALESH: Don't.
> Give up is not brave.
NATALIA: No.

*Natalia looks at the big tree. Pause.*

ALESH: Want some coffee?

*Indicates trailer.*

    I have.

NATALIA: Oh great. Sure.

ALESH: One minute.

*He goes inside. Natalia breaks off some needles and smells them. There is a little noise in the trailer: kitchen things.*

NATALIA: Good.

*Alesh comes out with the mugs of coffee from before. He hands Natalia the one he was drinking from.*

ALESH: Is. From home, from my village. Gift of my mother. I put sugar, ok?

NATALIA: Definitely.

ALESH: We drink in small cups. But: America: big.

NATALIA: There's small cups here too.

ALESH: Yes. I know.

*Alesh drinks. Natalia drinks.*

NATALIA: Oh wow.

ALESH: Thank you.

    Please sit! In the…

*Beat.*

    Forest.

*Natalia sits. Alesh sits.*

NATALIA: How is this?

*Alesh nods.*

ALESH: Yah. Ok. My first time to do it. So, "We'll See."

NATALIA: The guy your partner, he's been here other years.

ALESH: Yes. You remember?

NATALIA: But not you I know 'cause I would—

Yeah.

*Alesh drinks. Natalia drinks.*

ALESH: Gregor has being here seven years. He wants partner. Younger. Strong. Have the same...

*Native language:*

desire?

*English:*

we want the same.

NATALIA: What? *(i.e. "the same what?")*

ALESH: I don't know how to say.

You live here, many years?

NATALIA: I grew up here.

ALESH: Here?

NATALIA: In this neighborhood.

ALESH: That's nice.

NATALIA: It wasn't so nice then. I mean it was better. Because it was worse.

ALESH: You have job?

NATALIA: Oh

Yeah

Actually don't...really wanna...talk about that, if it's—

ALESH: Don't!

NATALIA: Everything is

*She drinks. She keeps her face down longer than she should. Alesh leans in.*

ALESH: You're a mouse in my hand.

You're safe.

*She picks up her face, wiping her eyes, and sniffles.*

NATALIA: Sorry.

ALESH: Ok.

*She's done crying.*

NATALIA: Sorry.

This is really nice of you. Do you do this a lot?

ALESH: What.

NATALIA: You must.

ALESH: Eh. No.

*She drinks.*

NATALIA: I'll never fall asleep tonight.

ALESH: May/be not—

NATALIA: You know that they used to say "stranger killers"?

*Beat.*

In like the seventies. Before we were born.

*Beat.*

Stranger, killers.

Huh.

ALESH: I don't know what is that.

NATALIA: Like last year. —You weren't here. So, last year at christmastime there were these murders. And it turned out that this'd been going on for years, I think five? Christmases before that and they just hadn't told the public but last year it got out. It was a big deal.

ALESH: Ah.

NATALIA: Gregor

would know about it.

Everyone did. The whole city. It was tremendous. The Christmas Ripper. It was...

ALESH: Did they
    Find him?
NATALIA: He's at large. Or she.
ALESH: She?

    *He relaxes.*

    Could be.
NATALIA: I keep ho—ha, expecting to see something in the newspaper, but. I
    guess he's laying low or, he's gone?
ALESH: You think about this, very much? Is not healthy.
NATALIA: It's not just me.
ALESH: But. Is...depressed.

    *Natalia drinks.*

NATALIA: Can I ask you a question?
ALESH: Yes, ok.
NATALIA: What's it like?

    *Beat.*

ALESH: What is.
NATALIA: Being...
    Handsome. Being as handsome as you are.
    I'm not, I'm just asking.
ALESH: Drink your coffee.

    *Natalia starts to stand.*

NATALIA: Shit, I'm sorry, I—
ALESH: Sit.

    *Beat. Natalia sits back down.*

    And drink the rest. Now.

    *Natalia drinks the rest of the coffee.*

You know why?

*She looks at him.*

I put drug.

NATALIA: In this?

ALESH: To make you to sleep.

*Natalia starts to stand again. Alesh pushes her back down.*

Sit. Don't be loud. This is forest.

*Natalia starts to feel the drug very strongly. She talks softly.*

NATALIA: This thing, listen, it won't be good for you. It's already such a mess. It literally doesn't even work half the time. It's rife with disease—

ALESH: Shhh Natalia.

NATALIA: That's my name.

I guessed.

*She passes out. He picks her up and carries her behind the trailer.*

*Gregor enters with a scary knife.*

*Alesh comes back.*

*Gregor hands Alesh the knife.*

*Alesh turns to go back behind the trailer.*

*He can't. He comes back. He passes the knife back to Gregor.*

ALESH: I...

GREGOR: You stand out here for us and look luminous.

*Gregor goes into the trailer.*

*Alesh stands outside. He looks beautiful.*

*After a while Gregor comes back out. He is holding Natalia's scarf.*

*They stand outside.*

# Part Two. We've Got the Law On Our Side

## Scene 0

*Nelly, a lady, finds some guy clothes. For example, a sweatshirt and knit cap. These could be clothes Alesh was wearing in Part One.*

*She picks them up and looks at them. Where did they come from? Whose are they?*

*She puts them on. Now she is Nally.*

*Nally exits.*

## Scene 1

*Alpert and Greggins are police detectives. They are at a crime scene.*

ALPERT: This guy is fucked.

GREGGINS: He prob'ly saw it on TV.

ALPERT: Doesn't mean he's not fucked.

GREGGINS: Anything look familiar?

ALPERT: Aa I don't watch that crap.

GREGGINS: Nah, remember last year same time?

ALPERT: Huh. You think it's that guy.

GREGGINS: Might be.

ALPERT: Could be I guess.

GREGGINS: You said the same exact thing then.

ALPERT: What, that the guy's fucked?

GREGGINS: Then again you say that a lot.

ALPERT: Not as much as I think it.

GREGGINS: 's not our job to judge. That's the judge's / job.

ALPERT: It's the jury's job.

GREGGINS: Yeah but I'm sayin, it's a distraction. I mean it's no good to ya in terms of the case.

ALPERT: Moral Outrage?

GREGGINS: Yeah, cause ya gotta / get inside his head.

ALPERT: "Get inside his head"? Ha. What was it, 'zact same M.O.?

GREGGINS: Close enough.

ALPERT: Slicer.

GREGGINS: That's right.

ALPERT: That's why they called him the uh—

GREGGINS: Yah.

ALPERT: Yeahb't Greg.

GREGGINS: Al?

ALPERT: See that every day almost. Practically.

GREGGINS: Look at her.

ALPERT: Yeah.

GREGGINS: Somethin's missing.

ALPERT: What. She's got all her fingers. Teeth. Can't see the toes.

GREGGINS: No, she's got her shoes on.

ALPERT: Yeah.

GREGGINS: Got her coat on.

ALPERT: Yeah.

GREGGINS: Her god damn coat is still on.

ALPERT: So.

GREGGINS: You got your coat on.

ALPERT: It's fuckin cold.

GREGGINS: Right.

ALPERT: So I got my coat on.

GREGGINS: Right, and?

ALPERT: And?

   *Beat.*

And a hat—

GREGGINS: Right.

ALPERT: Got a scarf—

GREGGINS: So where's hers?

ALPERT: Yeah, but Greggins, don'tcha think if she woulda prob'ly struggled, that stuff'd just come off?

GREGGINS: Could be. But what's he gonna do with it?

ALPERT: Toss it with the body. Uh-huh. I getcha.

GREGGINS: Unless—

ALPERT: Unless he's keepin it special.

GREGGINS: Same as last year.

ALPERT: Maybe he's got a sideline in winter accessories.

GREGGINS: Gently used.


## Scene 2

*Alpert and Greggins take off their coats etc. and are wearing gym clothes. They are at the gym. They work out while they talk.*

GREGGINS: You goin out to the Island again this year?

ALPERT: Funny thing. We always do, right?

GREGGINS: Heya Mike.

ALPERT: Mike. Since we been married, even before the kids, every year. Thanksgiving and Christmas Eve in Bay Ridge, Christmas Day on the Island.

GREGGINS: Traffic must be murder.

ALPERT: Oh it's terrible. But, y'allow for it, fine. Every year. So last night we're in bed, she's readin, I'm watchin the wrap-up, and outa nowhere I get the idea, I say hey Nell, why don't we stay home this year. We can make eggnog, the kids can play with their toys...

GREGGINS: Yeah.

ALPERT: You know we c' decorate the place, get a tree...

GREGGINS: Yeah so what'd / she

ALPERT: I say maybe we could ask Greggins if he wants to come over—anyway so she just immediately busts out cryin. Without a word. Just like suddenly cryin hysterically. In this way where she doesn't make any sound just her face is all stretched like a fuckin still shot from a horror movie.

So yeah I guess we're goin to the Island.

GREGGINS: What's the funny part?

ALPERT: What?

Oh, no, I just thought it was funny you askin today, it just happened last night, that's all.

*They work out.*

You got plans?

GREGGINS: Same as always.

ALPERT: Still haven't given it a shot, huh?

GREGGINS: What.

ALPERT: That…e-harmony.

Match dot com.

GREGGINS: Christ.

ALPERT: Sounds fun to me. Like shoppin for women on Amazon.

GREGGINS: That's sick.

ALPERT: It is not sick. All Nelly's single friends are on there.

GREGGINS: I'm not interested in Nelly's single friends.

ALPERT: No, I'm just sayin, it's

They got a broad base.

GREGGINS: I'll say.

ALPERT: That Anna's cute.

GREGGINS: Arright then.

*Greggins leaves.*

ALPERT: I don't want you ta be lonely.

I knew a guy once, this guy I knew

he couldn't uh
let's say he couldn't locate himself
ran screamin down the corridor of a plane he was s'posed ta be flyin
hadda lock'm outa the cockpit
an sit on'm.

I wasn't there but it sounds pretty rough. I'm just sayin. You gotta

commemorate your position every day afresh an it's hard ta keep your bearings if no one's there ta help. Well can be.

## Scene 3

*Interrogation. Nally is sitting in the room alone with a cup of coffee, the mug Natalia drank from in Part One. Pause. Alpert walks in, drying his hair with a towel. They look at each other. Alpert exits.*

NALLY: Hey!

*Pause. Greggins enters.*

GREGGINS: Mr. Nally. I'm detective Greggins. 'Preciate ya callin and comin in.
NALLY: Sure.

*Greggins sits. Pause.*

Can I get some cream for this?
GREGGINS: They didn't ask ya?

*Nally shakes his head.*

I'm sorry, they're usually pretty good about that.
NALLY: I'd drink it black but it takes a toll.

*Pause.*

This room gives you a feeling of being watched.

GREGGINS: So, Mr. Nally.

NALLY: Yes.

GREGGINS: You

would like

some cream.

NALLY: Please.

GREGGINS: wwAAAAAAGGGHHHHH!

*Pause. Nally fidgets.*

NALLY: What?

GREGGINS: You know what that is?

NALLY: Um

GREGGINS: That's what a victim feels. When she realizes she's been trapped. Drugged. By a man who is going to end her life now. And take everything. Everything. She's ever worked for. Hoped for. Take everything.

*Beat.*

I make this point.

NALLY: Ok, yeah.

GREGGINS: I make this point Mr. Nally because uh, it's important that you bear in mind the / gravity of what—

NALLY: I know, it's im/portant—

GREGGINS: Don't interrupt me.

NALLY: Sorry.

GREGGINS: Don't interrupt me.

*Pause.*

Now.

*Pause.*

NALLY: Well actually.

I really would like to feel sharp right now. Feel like I do need the coffee. So and the cream.

GREGGINS: Ya sleepy?

NALLY: A little tired.

GREGGINS: And why's that?

NALLY: It's that time of day. I usually have some coffee this time of day.

GREGGINS: It's not because you uh, didn't sleep too well last night.

NALLY: Think I slept ok.

GREGGINS: Weren't nervous about comin in here.

NALLY: Not, not nervous, no.

GREGGINS: No?

NALLY: I was curious.

GREGGINS: Curious what we'd ask ya?

NALLY: What it would be like.

GREGGINS: What's it like?

*Pause.*

NALLY: Look if, you tell me where it is...

GREGGINS: What the fuck is wrong with you? I got addicts in here alla time, you're like one a the worst I / ever saw.

NALLY: I just,

GREGGINS: DON'T INTERRUPT ME

*Beat.*

NALLY: I just when I identify something that I, feel that I need it's, I have a hard time getting past it. Putting it out of my mind, it's hard for me.

GREGGINS: You're compulsive.

NALLY: I don't know.

GREGGINS: You seen anyone about that?

NALLY: Nah.

GREGGINS: You gotta watch that.

NALLY: Yeah.

*Alpert enters, casually tossing a packet of cream up in the air and catching it.*

ALPERT: Yo.

GREGGINS: What's it like out there.

ALPERT: Wasteland.

*Alpert tosses the cream to Nally, who opens it and pours it into his coffee. Alpert sits down.*

GREGGINS: Odd guy, this guy.

ALPERT: That right?

GREGGINS: Uncontrollable Impulses.

ALPERT: Oh Really.

NALLY: No, not really.

ALPERT: Really.

GREGGINS: Who the fuck knows.

NALLY: I haven't been being uncooperative. You haven't asked me anything.

GREGGINS: We're just gettin goin.

ALPERT: Sorry if I held ya up.

*Pause. Nally drinks coffee. Pause.*

NALLY: Are we done?

GREGGINS: So. Mr. Nally.

NALLY: Uh-huh.

GREGGINS: You are the man that lives opposite.

ALPERT: Opposite—

GREGGINS: Opposite the lot.

NALLY: Yah.

GREGGINS: What
	is your occupation?

NALLY: You have it I thought.
	Copy.

ALPERT: Like the Kinky's?

NALLY: No, I...

GREGGINS: Copy, like ad copy.

NALLY: Yeah, I make the descriptions in catalogs. Like Brighten Someone's Holiday Season with our Colorful Gift Tin. Packed with Fun and Flavor.

ALPERT: What's that?

NALLY: Aplets and Cotlets.

GREGGINS: The fuck's that?

NALLY: A kinda candy from the Pacific Northwest.

ALPERT: I had it.

GREGGINS: And you work on this at home.

NALLY: Yah.

So on Tuesday night, I was sitting at my desk by the window, and I was looking out at the vacant lot across the street.

GREGGINS: Ya like that lot?

NALLY: Do I like it?

GREGGINS: Yeah, 's it a feature a the environment that so for instance helped sell ya on livin there?

NALLY: I don't think it was vacant when I moved there. It was something else. I don't remember.

GREGGINS: That's right. It was a House a Pancakes.

NALLY: Right.

GREGGINS: Ya like pancakes?

NALLY: Yes.

*Greggins and Alpert exchange a glance.*

ALPERT: When you say Tuesday Night, you mean Wednesday morning?

NALLY: Yeah, that's right.

ALPERT: Bout what time?

NALLY: Two. Around two I guess.

GREGGINS: And you were lookin out the window at the lot.

NALLY: Well. The thing about the lot is. I've seen stuff there before.

GREGGINS: What kinda stuff?

*Beat.*

NALLY: Animals.

GREGGINS: Animals.

NALLY: Yeah.

GREGGINS: Dogs?

ALPERT: Cats.

NALLY: Wild animals.

ALPERT: Raccoons?

NALLY: No. Well. Raccoons aren't that big though.

ALPERT: How big?

NALLY: I don't know. Like a…

GREGGINS: Coyotes.

NALLY: No.

ALPERT: (*To Greggins*) Coyotes? In the city, are you fuckin kidding me?

NALLY: They're not coyotes.

GREGGINS: They been sighted.

ALPERT: No way.

NALLY: It's a totally different shape.

ALPERT: They got bears in Detroit.

NALLY: Low to the ground.

ALPERT: Got wild pigs in Berlin.

GREGGINS: Ok. Did you see 'em on Wednesday morning? Tuesday night?

NALLY: No. I only ever saw them once.

*Beat.*

GREGGINS: So arright.

ALPERT: They predators?

NALLY: I think they're scavengers.

GREGGINS: Arright. Excuse me. Ok?

ALPERT: Yeah.

GREGGINS: Ok.

ALPERT: Two o'clock. Wednesday morning.

NALLY: I see two guys across the street carrying something into the lot.

ALPERT & GREGGINS: Two guys.

*They look at each other.*

You sure 'bout that?

NALLY: Pretty sure.

GREGGINS: Describe these men.

NALLY: It was pretty dark.

ALPERT: Tall, short, fat.

NALLY: I think one of them was a little smaller than the other. Not fat. They were wearing bulky jackets. And hats, I think they were both wearing caps. Knit caps.

GREGGINS: Men's caps.

NALLY: Yeah. They were men.

GREGGINS: Complexion?

ALPERT: White guys, black guys...

NALLY: Oh, I don't know. I really couldn't tell.

GREGGINS: You couldn't tell? You been livin in this city...

NALLY: Twelve years

GREGGINS: Twelve years, you can't tell the difference how a black guy walks from how a white guy?

NALLY: I don't

ALPERT: He's bein sensitive. Listen—

GREGGINS: Listen. The best thing you can do for mankind right now is tell us everything you thought you saw.

NALLY: Well I guess I prob'ly thought they were white.

ALPERT: What about any peculiarity in the way they were walkin. Like a limp.

NALLY: Well, when they came they were carrying the, bag, so, it was heavy so, they were both walking like people who're carrying something heavy. It was that long kind of duffle bag.

GREGGINS: We got the bag.

NALLY: I saw them walk into the lot, and towards the back and into the dark. And then I couldn't see them. And then they came out of the dark without the bag, they left the lot and they walked—

*Pause.*

ALPERT: You rememberin somethin?

*Beat.*

NALLY: They embraced.

At the edge of the lot they stopped and embraced. And then they walked away to the east.

ALPERT: When you say Embraced.

GREGGINS: They hug?

NALLY: No, it. Was like a dance.

ALPERT & GREGGINS: A dance?

NALLY: They were like one thing. A thing and its shadow. Like they'd been practicing. But maybe

*Beat.*

Maybe I just imagined that.

*End of scene. Nally takes off his guy things and becomes Nelly, Alpert's wife.*


## Scene 4

*Greggins and Nelly at Nelly and Alpert's house. Post-coitus. Silence.*

GREGGINS: What'd you do this morning?

NELLY: I don't know.

I literally don't know what I did. The kids went to school...

GREGGINS: Maybe you should think about goin back to work.

NELLY: Did my husband say something?

GREGGINS: No. Al...no.

NELLY: He thinks I'm with my friend Sandra. Sandra moved to Texas seven years ago.

GREGGINS: Jesus, Nell. Be careful.

NELLY: That face of his.

*Pause.*

Greg?

This um, this latest …murders—

GREGGINS: Nell–

NELLY: He doesn't wanna talk about it either. No one will talk to me about it but I really would like to.

GREGGINS: Why?

NELLY: I'm afraid I'm gonna blurt it out with the kids.

GREGGINS: Why, what's so interesting?

NELLY: It's not interesting. It just reminds me of myself.

GREGGINS: The Christmas Ripper. Yourself.

NELLY: No. I don't know.

GREGGINS: It's not a movie.

NELLY: I fucking know it's not a movie. God, it's like the two of you're quoting from the same manual.

GREGGINS: Well.

NELLY: I think you feel guilty when we meet so you unconsciously try to be as much like him as possible. So then it'll be him here instead of you.

GREGGINS: Course I feel guilty.

NELLY: Me too.

GREGGINS: In fact I want…

*Beat.*

I wanna wound myself. I wanna shoot off my foot.

NELLY: Gross.

GREGGINS: Get a tattoo across my face. I wanna sell my body as a punching bag.

NELLY: Huh.

GREGGINS: You too?

NELLY: He's your partner.

GREGGINS: You don't wanna go home with some guy at a bar so he can drug you and cut your throat and take off with your winter wear?

NELLY: My what?

GREGGINS: Yeah leave your corpse in a dumpster or a vacant lot where every dweeb in the neighborhood can jerk off on ya while ya decompose or get... eaten by some kinda imaginary urban wildlife before it slinks across the river to Jersey and parcels out your ribs for its pups or kats or cubs or whateverthefuck

Well isn't that what you're talkin about? That's what you wanna talk about?

NELLY: Why are you angry at me?

GREGGINS: I'm not.

NELLY: It sounds like you're yelling at me.

GREGGINS: I'm not.

NELLY: I did have a dream I'd like to discuss.

*Greggins puts his head in his hands.*

GREGGINS: Yeah?

NELLY: You're making a goddamn scene.

GREGGINS: What Was The Dream

NELLY: Well I think it might upset you.

GREGGINS: No, please.

NELLY: I dreamt that Al—

I dreamt that Al had had this family tradition I didn't know about, where the men would actually dress up in santa suits on Christmas Eve and sit up in the living room all night. Not doing anything, just sitting there on the divan. Al was telling me this and I thought it was funny he hadn't ever mentioned it but he said the time wasn't right 'til now. He had the suit, up in the closet in the bedroom. And I thought it's, y'know, maybe it's not a great place for it up there. So I said well let's, can I see it. And he said wait, I'll put it on. And then he was in the bedroom, I was waiting outside, he had the door locked and I could hear him moving around in there and then he said, You ready? And uh, he opened the door.

And the suit was not a santa suit. It was black, all black, even the beard. I said it's gone rotten, it's all black, take it off, you'll get sick. He said it's not black, look. And he was right, it was just dark red, very dark red, and it was soaking wet. He said this is how you have to keep it. Only his voice didn't sound like him, it was like he had an accent now a Polish or Russian, he said do you like it? Only then it wasn't him anymore, it was you.

*Pause.*

GREGGINS: Santa's Christmas Slay. A-Y. Nineteen eighty-five.

You musta seen it.

NELLY: Of course I never saw it.

GREGGINS: Yeah, evidently you did, you just don't remember.

NELLY: I don't believe that what I just described is from a movie.

GREGGINS: The crusty old suit? Yeah.

*Greggins gets dressed.*

NELLY: Are you in that movie?

Because Greg, I think I'm noticing something. There's kinda like a pattern. Or a, circle. A cycle.

GREGGINS: Like a dance, he said. Like a thing and its shadow.

NELLY: I think we might be wrong when we call each other by names.

GREGGINS: "Embraced."

NELLY: And so you and Al for instance,

GREGGINS: "Embraced."

NELLY: you're the same event, just laid out at different points in space and time.

GREGGINS: "Animals." Fuckin nut job.

NELLY: Who?

GREGGINS: Doesn't matter.

NELLY: That's what I'm saying. I think a serial killer—it's still called that?

GREGGINS: Yeah.

NELLY: I think someone like that...is reacting to this same thing I'm having, this perception that there's no difference between different people. So, you do it once, you do it again...

GREGGINS: There's usually a type.

NELLY: Right.

GREGGINS: You're saying you have a type?

NELLY: No, no.

*Beat.*

GREGGINS: Is there someone else?

NELLY: There's no one else. That's what I'm saying.

## Scene 5

*Alpert at the office, on the phone.*

ALPERT: Time a death? Uh-huh.

Multiple stab.

Evidence a yeah, uh-huh.

And no coat. Nothin! I see. Yeah. No. Dom, I really doubt if it's one of ours. Thanks for the tip though. Hey Dom.

Whataya gettin Mary for Christmas.

*Greggins enters.*

Uh. That's nice.

Yeeeah I don't know, I can't decide.

Arright, take care.

GREGGINS: Hey pal.

ALPERT: Hey "pal."

GREGGINS: What?

ALPERT: Pal.

*Greggins sits at his desk.*

GREGGINS: Been thinkin about that freak.

ALPERT: Nally?

GREGGINS: What? Yeah.

ALPERT: Think he's fulla shit?

GREGGINS: I don't know.

ALPERT: Team a two.

GREGGINS: Aplets and Grotlets.

ALPERT: What?

GREGGINS: Partnership in general Al, it's a fucked-up thing, no offense.

ALPERT: Whatta you know, bachelor?

GREGGINS: Nothin.
He's gonna strike again, he's got ten days til Christmas and we got nothin.
We got the law on our side. That used to be an expression around here. Like
code for We got jack shit.

ALPERT: That's funny.

GREGGINS: Lieutenant made us cut it out, said it fucked morale.

ALPERT: We got the law on our side.

GREGGINS: Bleak and Lawless Land.

ALPERT: Flocks of, flocks / of—

GREGGINS: Herds

ALPERT: Waves and—

GREGGINS: Tumble/weeds

ALPERT: Tumbleweeds of / despair

GREGGINS: God, it's a fuckin / nightmare

ALPERT: You just reach into the barrel and take them.

GREGGINS: Rake your fingers through the mud and there they are, rotten and luscious.

ALPERT: Numbered are the days.

GREGGINS: Take them. Shit.

ALPERT: Shit.

GREGGINS: Had a dream last night you were wearin a santa suit.

ALPERT: Yeah?

GREGGINS: Yeah, it was a tradition in your family.

ALPERT: That's funny.

GREGGINS: Yeah it was this crazy eastern thing. It was black. It was for a funeral.

ALPERT: You're kiddin.

GREGGINS: You had it in your closet.

ALPERT: I thought I was wearin it.

GREGGINS: Yeah. No. I was wearin it.

*Beat.*

ALPERT: It's funny because I do have a suit like that.

GREGGINS: You mean a black suit.

ALPERT: No.

*Pause.*

You know sometimes...

GREGGINS: What.

ALPERT: Nothin.

# Scene 6

*Nelly at home. Alpert comes in from outside.*

NELLY: Hi baby.
ALPERT: Hi "baby."
NELLY: What.
ALPERT: Baby.
NELLY: What?
ALPERT: Huh.

*Nelly tries to take his coat. He shrugs violently away.*

NELLY: Take your / hat?
ALPERT: No.
NELLY: You wanna keep 'em on?

*Beat.*

ALPERT: Freezing.
NELLY: I'll turn the heat up.
ALPERT: No. Out there.
NELLY: "It's a wasteland."
ALPERT: Who said that?
NELLY: What?
    I did.

*Alpert sniffs the air.*

ALPERT: The fuck's that.

*Nelly sniffs.*

NELLY: Um. Chops? They're havin a sale.
ALPERT: Who's.
NELLY: Animal. Some animal.

ALPERT: Smells great.

*Beat.*

What'd you do today?

NELLY: Y'know.

ALPERT: Nope.

NELLY: Y'do.

ALPERT: Nope, nope.

NELLY: Infid—

ALPERT: Nell—

NELLY: Infideliss, -icity

ALPERT: Whattaya talkin about, shut up.

NELLY: Yup.

ALPERT: Christ.

NELLY: Handsome. Fuck /

you.

ALPERT: Just

don't tell other people our secrets please.

NELLY: We have secrets?

ALPERT: Yeah. Yeah, pretty much everything that passes between us is a secret, Nell, is the assumption I woulda made. And double for stuff you find out on your own.

NELLY: I don't know what you're referring to.

ALPERT: My santa suit?

NELLY: Your what?

ALPERT: I told you, when I was a…kid or somethin? Fuck. Forget it.

NELLY: No. You tell me nothing! What is your secret?

ALPERT: Has nothin t'do with me.

NELLY: Tell me your secret! It will bind me to you.

ALPERT: Ha, my secret?

I stabbed my wife in the chest eighteen times.

NELLY: Your wife me?

ALPERT: And in the eyes. Through the soles of her feet. Behind her knees. There was ribbons of blood,

but.

NELLY: Yeah?

ALPERT: It was mostly just a message. To my friend.

*Alpert leaves.*

NELLY: Last night I woke up and found that I was not at home. And I was not wearing my own clothes. And then I wasn't sure. Maybe they were my clothes, and I was someone else. But I could find no information on this, within me or without.

I don't know whose friend once said it took her a long time to realize who she was and what she wanted.

Who you are?

What you want?

Gulls sweep the air.

I walked in these stranger-clothes, through this place I didn't recognize, in the night. A different part of the city, or a different city, near a highway. Everything was huge, had been built for machines, not people, and there were no windows anywhere, no doors. I thought I should try to get back, to get to someplace I could get back from. I thought this was why I was walking. And then I realized no. I was heading further into this place. I was trying to get to its exact center.

*Nelly has become Nally. He exits.*

# Scene 7

*At the exact center. Alpert and Greggins in an action sequence.*

GREGGINS: Police!

    *Alpert and Greggins kick down the door. They move through the space cautiously.*

ALPERT: Clear.

GREGGINS: Clear. Arright.

    *They crouch.*

ALPERT: I never seen this place.

GREGGINS: Don'tcha remember what I told ya when we first got partnered up?

ALPERT: That the worst mistake is to think you know the city.

GREGGINS: Remember that Night Club?

ALPERT: Yeah. What about it. Arright.

    Jesus, shut up.

GREGGINS: What's eatin you?

ALPERT: Nothin.

GREGGINS: Perfect spot.

ALPERT: Yeah, I'd give it a go.

GREGGINS: What.

ALPERT: Life a crime.

GREGGINS: Have to be crazy.

ALPERT: Yeah, well.

    *Time passes.*

GREGGINS: 'At's not what I asked ya.

ALPERT: What'd you ask me?

GREGGINS: Where ya from.

ALPERT: You been there.

GREGGINS: No, yer people. Originally.

ALPERT: Y'know everything had different names a hundred years ago.

"Alpert" that's some kinda alteration. I don't know from what.

Y'I told Nelly we could change it.

GREGGINS: What?

ALPERT: Yeah, I don't know, I thought, be more fair, we both change. But.

GREGGINS: Must be strange, have a new name in the middle of your life.

ALPERT: Yeah.

GREGGINS: Belong to someone.

ALPERT: Well.

GREGGINS: Lucky.

ALPERT: Yeah I am?

GREGGINS: She is. Wait!

*Alpert and Greggins hear something.*

ALPERT: Wheresat?

GREGGINS: Overthere.

*They move over to a doorway.*

ALPERT: Holy shit.

GREGGINS: Get down.

*They crouch.*

See 'em? They can't see us, see 'em?

ALPERT: Two white guys with coats and hats like he said.

GREGGINS: He said dancin.

ALPERT: They ain't dancin.

GREGGINS: Listen.

*They listen.*

The handsome one, what's he sayin?

ALPERT: Somethin about datin on the internet.

GREGGINS: You sure?

ALPERT: And now the ugly one's sayin…

how he's been sleepin with the handsome one's wife
and how

GREGGINS: Nah, they're speakin like Russian or—

ALPERT: And how the handsome one better keep in line

GREGGINS: like Albani-Slovakian-Polish—

ALPERT: Cause the ugly one's got powerful fuckin friends who was the one who burned down the handsome one's village in the first place out a—

GREGGINS: Al, grip that shit.

ALPERT: Out a sheer envy a his superior frame and good nature

GREGGINS: Horseshit, they got knives out. Police!

*Greggins exits at a run, drawing his gun. Alpert doesn't join him.*

*There are two gunshots.*

*Pause.*

*Greggins enters, staggering. He has a knife in his back.*

ALPERT: Ya get 'em?

GREGGINS: One of 'em.

*Greggins falls. Pause.*

ALPERT: I have a face and a neck and a body that hurts men's hearts.

One look, one look and they're broken.
This city is totally mine.
It's gonna be superior.

*Nally enters.*

NALLY: More light. Better music.

ALPERT: The food'll be folded by hand.

NALLY: More nourishing.

ALPERT: Nell?

NALLY: Don't call me that anymore. We'll live in spirals. Copying the copies of copies of a crime that never happened.

ALPERT: That we only dreamed.

NALLY: We don't need names. Not the regular kind.

*They take each other's hand and walk away.*

*Lights up on Greggins, stirring. Greggins gasps.*

GREGGINS: Al?

*Sounds that are not the sounds of a city: mountain wilderness sounds. Greggins gets up onto his elbows. He sees something.*

The fuck?

Is that a dog?

That's not a dog.

*Sound of a creature approaching.*

What are you? Raccoon?

No.

You...

I wanna talk to you.

Come

closer.

*Greggins loses consciousness.*

*Sound of a creature approaching nearer.*

*Sound of a creature eating.*

# Part Three. The Lesser Pandas

*Alfo and Noplop are red pandas. They are hanging out in a vacant lot. Alfo is reading the paperback from Part One, upside-down. Then he starts eating the paperback. Noplop tries to get in on it and they tussle, then separate. Pause.*

NOPLOP: Do you
    have a sense memory
    of the Himalayas?

ALFO: Uh…

NOPLOP: I have a feeling it was colder there. Because it's very cold here and but I'm not cold at all.

ALFO: You remember that?

NOPLOP: I don't know. It might just be common knowledge.

ALFO: How would you get your paws on common knowledge?

NOPLOP: How indeed.

ALFO: You're really not cold at all?

NOPLOP: No. Why, are you?

ALFO: No.

  *Pause.*

  This vacant lot smells like pancakes.

NOPLOP: Do you have a sense memory of the Zoo?

ALFO: I don't understand that expression.

  *Alfo rolls on his back. Pause.*

  Can you see him?

NOPLOP: Yeah. He's going for it.

ALFO: And?

NOPLOP: Looks ok.

ALFO: Well let's give it a minute anyway.

NOPLOP: I'm not super hungry. I had all that
    popcorn.

ALFO: You gotta be careful.

NOPLOP: No one saw. They were throwing it away!

ALFO: I don't wanna become some kind of local color.

NOPLOP: They don't have that here.

ALFO: Who knows what they have here. It's a paradise of perversions.

NOPLOP: He's coming over.

*Grox the panda enters. He is gnawing on a bloody bone.*

ALFO: Hey.

GROX: Hey.

NOPLOP: Hey.

GROX: Hey.

*Grox gnaws the bone. Noplop and Alfo watch surreptitiously. For a while.*

ALFO: How is it?

GROX: It's all right.

NOPLOP: I lucked out a couple hours ago behind the cineplex.

GROX: Oh yeah?

NOPLOP: Whole garbage bag full of popcorn.

GROX: Yum.

    I like those Twizzle-ers.

NOPLOP: What's that?

GROX: Hard to explain. I'll bring you one next time I get some.

NOPLOP: Cool. Thanks.

ALFO: Just all right?

GROX: It don't have that sweetness they sometimes have.

NOPLOP: You've got a real sweet tooth.

GROX: Every bone in my body, baby.

ALFO: It's only sweet when it's rotten. That one's fresh. And they're gonna be coming for it and they're gonna get curious about whose teethmarks that is.

GROX: Yeah, they'll think it's a Roffer you know. There's all different kinds of Roffers.

NOPLOP: Don't I know it.

GROX: What, you had a run-in?

ALFO: She sure did.

NOPLOP: He was no joke either. But he was on a—

*She mimes being on a leash.*

thing.

GROX: So they saw you!

ALFO & NOPLOP: No.

NOPLOP: I was behind the cans. Roffer saw me but the human wasn't in on it. And you know they don't talk. Isn't that weird? Can you imagine living with someone you couldn't talk to?

GROX: Depends on who.

*Grox gnaws the bone sumptuously for her benefit.*

Wanna bite?

*Noplop looks at Alfo.*

ALFO: I'll try it.

GROX: Didn't ask you, man. There's plenty over there.

NOPLOP: No, I'm full.

GROX: She wants it, man. Go pick her up a riblet.

ALFO: It makes us conspicuous.

GROX: This is some tedium. I'm gonna go snout out an eye.

NOPLOP: What if the Roffers killed him? Maybe they're rising.

GROX: It doesn't smell like that. Don't smell them on it. This is natural causes. Human on human.

ALFO: They're definitely coming for this one. Grox, lay off it pal, please.

GROX: Ordinarily Alfo I'd do you that favor, but. There was something about him, something about him that I really connected to, and I'll tell you, I got a distinct sense he was delivering us a gift.

ALFO: Aw, shut—

GROX: No, I'm serious.

*Alfo wanders off and discovers the radio from Part One.*

> His demeanor, and. The way he looked through the shadows. It felt like, I got the feeling he was looking right at me, and he kinda...laid himself out, like. A tribute. Real respectful. And I tell you what else, I think he's been watching us for a while. From that thing way across there.

*They look out towards the audience.*

NOPLOP: Is that his nest?

ALFO: I don't see anything.

*Alfo tinkers with the radio.*

GROX: He lurked in the dark. Like us.

NOPLOP: How can you tell it's a He?

GROX: Like I said, we connected.

NOPLOP: Huh.

> *The radio starts to play. Music: an upbeat shuffle. Noplop addresses the audience.*

NOPLOP: I have a sense memory.

> What it was like before having a body.
> What it was like just being the wind, a killer wind assailing the world and chomping brute matter into zilch
> And if you assail me I would assail you raarr right back, right back
> Then all this other stuff happened...

ALFO & GROX: When I said you looked exactly like your mother like exactly

> I didn't mean to hurt your feelings
> She's my mother too, or I think so
> And anyway it's been a while since I've seen her.

NOPLOP: Hey losers!

ALFO & GROX: Yes!

NOPLOP: I wanna propose a new paradigm.

ALFO & GROX: Ok!

NOPLOP: We take turns seducing the humans and slaughtering them. By way of the big blood vessel in the neck. We cover them up with choice garbage and snack throughout the week, allowing the flavors to meld.

ALFO & GROX: Ok!

NOPLOP: After all, we're still attractive.

ALFO & GROX: Ok!

NOPLOP: OUR QUALITY OF LIFE WILL SKYROCKET

GROX: Ok!

ALFO: Not really though.

NOPLOP: What.

ALFO: Not really will we do this thing.

NOPLOP: Why?

GROX: As a paradigm it's fine.

ALFO: It's noble and beautiful. But it leaves me cold.

GROX: This isn't some utopia.

NOPLOP: Know why they call us the Lesser Pandas?

ALFO: Obviously.

NOPLOP: Wrong. You're wrong.

GROX: It's cause of our stature.

NOPLOP: No, wrong.

*Grox and Alfo panda around.*

But who cares actually?
Pretty soon the same catastrophe that drove us here will drive us out.
Better not to invest too much in any one thing. I have a feeling
the next place'll be similar to this one.

*The music goes out.*

Except
this whole time there's something seething

I used to think it would go away
but at times like this I feel it more than ever
it's pouring through me right now though you don't notice and that
ignorance will be your downfall, "friends."

*Everyone freezes.*

*Noplop raises a red panda twitter with her voice.*

*Grox and Alfo join in. It is a very eerie sound.*

*They stop.*

*Pause.*

*They do it again.*

*They stop.*

Woe to you if you think this is not in my deepest blood.


*THE END*

# Dreamless Land

These notions of forebears, of houses where lamps are lit at night, and other such, where do they come to me from?

—Samuel Beckett, *The Unnamable*

*Dreamless Land* was first produced by New York City Players at the Abrons Arts Center in November 2011. It was directed by the author. The performers were Linda Mancini, Jenny Seastone, Richard Toth, and Ben Williams. Set design was by Jason Simms, costume design by Mia Bienovich, lighting design by Ben Kato, and sound design by Bobby McElver; the associate sound designer was Cooper Gardner; Producer, Richard Maxwell; Associate Producer, Lindsay Hockaday; Production Stage Manager, Amy Groeschel.

## Characters

Joyce, a grown-up woman
Carver, a grown-up man
Morton, 15, later Martin, 25
Haley, 15 and 25

## Notes

The center of the stage is occupied by a large, futuristic Cube, which serves as a table, a TV, and a source of information (for the characters) throughout. The audience never sees any of the images it displays.

Three seats are placed around the stage: one to stage left, one to stage right, one downstage. Except on one occasion, "exit" means that a character goes and sits in one of these seats. The seats can also be moved onto the stage for scenes as needed. Haley never leaves the stage in Part One.

A slash / in a line indicates that the following line starts at this point and overlaps with this one.

## Scene 0: Haley

*Carver, Joyce and Morton are seated around the stage.*

*Haley enters.*

*She looks at Carver.*

*She looks at Joyce.*

*She looks at Morton.*

*She chooses:*

*Morton gets a propeller beanie.*

*Haley chooses:*

*Scary music starts to play. Haley sits down, in an upstage corner, to watch.*

# Part One

## Scene 1: Back Story. Poltergeist Amityville Shining

*Scary music. Morton enters in a propeller beanie, with a teddy bear: he's little. He sees the Cube. He walks around it, then plops down in front of it, fascinated.*

*The music becomes cheerful. A sunny day in the suburbs. Joyce and Carver enter, holding hands. Haley is watching.*

JOYCE: Oh, Carver, it's…
CARVER: What?
JOYCE: Thank you.

*Joyce kisses Carver on the cheek.*

CARVER: That's all I get? For a whole house?
JOYCE: Hey, you get the house too.
CARVER: No kidding. I told you, a wine cellar.
JOYCE: Yeah, about fifty times. Since when are you interested in wine?
CARVER: When a man reaches a certain age … becomes a homeowner…
JOYCE: Ok gramps. Where's Morton?

*They find Morton by the Cube.*

CARVER: Hey little man.
JOYCE: Hey baby, what'd you find?
MORTON: Look, Daddy!

*Morton shows Carver something on the back of the Cube. Carver and Joyce lean in to look. The lights go out.*

*Lights come back on. Morton is sitting by the cube, playing. Joyce and Carver are sitting around.*

JOYCE: How was school?

MORTON: Ok.

JOYCE: What's Miss Throat like?

MORTON: She's nice.

JOYCE: What are you learning about?

MORTON: Nave 'mericans.

*Haley giggles.*

JOYCE: Oh really? That's interesting.

*Pause.*

How are the other kids?

CARVER: Jesus Christ!

JOYCE: What's wrong?

CARVER: Didn't realize this was an interrogation chamber.

JOYCE: I'm not interrogating him. Was I Morton?

CARVER: Leave him alone! Will you leave him alone? He's playing firetrucks.

MORTON: They're ambulances, Daddy.

JOYCE: You could be an ambulance driver when you grow up. Ernest Hemingway, that's your Dad's most favorite writer, he was an ambulance driver during World War One.

CARVER: Or you could be an ambulance chaser like your uncle.

JOYCE: Jack isn't an ambulance chaser.

CARVER: Imagine that, Morton. Someone gets his leg crushed under a subway train—

JOYCE: That's enough!

CARVER: He loves it! That's what boys like, Joyce. Blood and pus and crunching bones and screaming. Right, Morton?

MORTON: I'on't know.

CARVER: Come on, Morton, you can tell Mommy.

JOYCE: Now who's interrogating?

CARVER: SHUT THE FUCK UP!

*He gets up.*

I'll be in the cellar.

*He exits.*

*Pause.*

JOYCE: Oh, sometimes moving to a new place makes people stressed out because there's so much for them to do. He'll feel better soon.

MORTON: Do you still love him?

JOYCE: Of course.

*Lights dim. Carver and Joyce go to sleep. Morton converses with the Cube.*

MORTON: Wha'd' you mean?

I wish you would talk normal so I could understand.

What's "tongs"?

Oh.

Does it hurt?

No thass OK.

No I don't wanna.

No I SAID NO!

*Morton is upset. Haley picks up Morton's teddy bear and hands it to him.*

Thank you.

*Morton falls asleep.*

*The bedroom: Joyce and Carver are asleep. Carver has a wine bottle beside him. Infernal noises start. Carver's hands slowly rise. As if of their own accord, they take a strangling position. Suddenly he wakes up and drops his hands.*

CARVER: No.

*The scary noises stop. Then start again. His hands move slowly back into the same position. This time Carver can't drop them.*

No!

*Joyce wakes up. She sees Carver's hands and jumps up.*

JOYCE: Carver!

CARVER: Joyce I—

*He is possessed.*

Where are you going, Joyce?

JOYCE: What are you doing? You're crazy!

CARVER: I've learned a lot down in the cellar of your new house.

JOYCE: Stay away!

CARVER: Stupid cunt. Retard son.

JOYCE: Morton!

CARVER: Morton.

JOYCE: You haven't—you wouldn't—

MORTON: Mommy?

JOYCE: Morton, I want you to go over to the neighbor's house—

*Carver chases Morton around the Cube. Morton talks to it.*

MORTON: Make my dad stop it.

You can I know you can.

No! Why would I do that? Stupid!

CARVER: Sometimes I have a hard time expressing my feelings.

JOYCE: Bastard!

CARVER: *(Normal voice)* But what you should remember is that I always—

*Joyce has been struggling to get hold of the wine bottle. Now she has it and is about to smash it on Carver's head.*

HALEY: No!

*Lights out. There is a smashing sound. Then lights come back up to normal and Dinosaur Jr.'s song "Feel The Pain" plays, and we are in...*

## Scene 2: Morton's Room

*Haley and Morton are fifteen. They are standing behind the Cube, playing "Feel the Pain" on Guitar Hero, with Haley on bass. They play for a while.*

MORTON: What?

    *They play more.*

HALEY: It was pretty brave.

MORTON: I wanna beat my score.

    *Pause while they play.*

        You gotta use the pedal.

    *They play.*

        Use the pedal!

HALEY: What pedal?

        Is he nice?

MORTON: Yeah, I guess.

HALEY: Does he talk like...

MORTON: Pretty normal.

HALEY: Yeah but, I mean does he sound like someone who works in an office? Or...

MORTON: He works in a freelance.

HALEY: I know, you said.

MORTON: So that's how he sounds.

HALEY: Next Friday?

MORTON: Friday the twenty-fifth.

HALEY: Are you gonna miss school?

MORTON: I guess.

HALEY: Your mom's gonna let you?

MORTON: She pretty much has to.

HALEY: Why does she have to?

*They finish the song. They see their scores.*

MORTON: Ninety-ssfuck.

HALEY: Is she mad?

MORTON: Maybe. Fuck.

HALEY: I'd be really mad.

I'd probably start poisoning your food so you'd get sick and couldn't go.

MORTON: She doesn't make my food.

HALEY: Or I'd hire someone, I'd hire one of those guys. Not for you, for him.

MORTON: What guys.

HALEY: From the back of the magazine. You know those guys in the magazine, we talked about it, you told me about it. The like "Bounty Hunters."

MORTON: Oh.

HALEY: I'd hire one of them to go after him and rough it up. Like get him against a wall and show him his gun and just hit him. And make him leave you alone. And say something to him like—

MORTON: Why would you hire someone? Why would you have to hire someone? Why wouldn't you just do it? You didn't even see those ads. You're so fucking lame.

*Morton taps the Cube to switch it to TV. We hear it very softly under the remaining dialogue.*

HALEY: My friend Morton is going to meet his dad for the first time. His dad has connections to a hotel in Las Vegas so he can hook them up with a cool place to stay. Legally Morton isn't old enough to go into the casinos or obviously the strip clubs but it'll be fun to dress up and try to fool everyone and anyway the dad has connections all over town. He says to Morton over the phone:

CARVER: I hear you've never been to Vegas.

HALEY: (*To Morton*) Like you wouldn't have to hire someone.

MORTON: Shut up. Get me another Squirt.

HALEY: You still have that one.

MORTON: Tastes weird.

HALEY: Squirt always tastes weird. That's why we like it.

Maybe we should switch.

MORTON: Gross.

HALEY: No!!! To another brand.

MORTON: There's Coca-Cola World there.

HALEY: It's an attraction?

MORTON: For seven dollars you can get sixteen kinds of soda from different countries.

HALEY: Fanta's from Germany. Hitler invented it.

MORTON: Not Fanta. Stuff you never heard of.

HALEY: I might've heard of it.

MORTON: I doubt that.

HALEY: What if he doesn't want to go there?

MORTON: Go by myself.

HALEY: What if he doesn't let you?

MORTON: It's not up to him.

HALEY: He might still think of you like a little kid.

MORTON: (*Violently*) Who wouldn't want to get sixteen kinds of sodas for seven dollars? That's a great deal.

HALEY: Yeah, you're right.

*Beat.*

You should bring me back some.

MORTON: They're in cups.

*They watch for a while. Haley gets weirded out and presses the button on the Cube. Lights and sound change. Music like the opening credits of a seventies James Bond movie: poppy and upbeat but slightly sinister.*

# Scene 3: From Russia With L---

*Joyce in her office at the S.H.A.R.P. syndicate. Haley enters. The music drops in volume.*

JOYCE: On the scale please.

    *Haley steps on a scale. It beeps.*

    Six over.

HALEY: I—

JOYCE: Off.

    *Haley steps off the scale.*

HALEY: The gym is closed for renovation. The past two weeks.

JOYCE: You should be using S.H.A.R.P. facilities.

HALEY: I don't think I have clearance.

    *Haley scans her wrist on the Cube. It beeps.*

JOYCE: Hm.

    I'm going to look into it. Shouldn't I?

    We do value your youth. Your appearance of youth. Your ductility. Now.

    *Joyce touches something to call up an image on the Cube.*

    This is Carver.

    Morton's dad.

HALEY: Oh.

JOYCE: That's right, take a long look.

    *Haley looks.*

    We've confirmed the DNA.

HALEY: I guess Morton could turn out like that. If he doesn't mess up too much.

JOYCE: You find him handsome?

HALEY: I guess.

JOYCE: He is.

HALEY: He is when he smiles.

JOYCE: Not Morton. His father.

HALEY: Oh. I see.

JOYCE: I want you to look at it until you feel the swelling of love.

*Haley looks for a long time.*

HALEY: Ok.

JOYCE: Now stop!

*Haley looks away.*

Look at me. What do you feel.

HALEY: About you?

JOYCE: Don't be stupid. What do you feel?

HALEY: The swelling of love for Morton's father.

JOYCE: Describe it.

HALEY: I feel that I would like to get to know him. And have him take me out to lunch. And on a train.

JOYCE: Yes.

HALEY: And think I was funny and cool.

JOYCE: That's fine.

*The picture goes out.*

Your work to date has been satisfactory.

HALEY: Ok.

JOYCE: "Satisfactory" is the top of our scale. No one is rated higher.

HALEY: Oh wow.

JOYCE: Because your work to date has been satisfactory, Number Forty-Seven, we're bumping you up to a new assignment level.

HALEY: Yesss!

JOYCE: In fact we bumped you up several months ago, but there was no reason to mention it.

HALEY: What's my—

*Joyce very quickly takes a knife out of a sheath on her garter belt and throws it at Haley. Haley dodges it and it flies offstage. Neither of them is surprised.*

JOYCE: You are to find Morton's father before he finds Morton and before Morton finds him; find Morton's father before Morton or his father finds you. The man is a high roller. Let's see how he does at...

*Joyce looks Haley up and down.*

mini-baccarat.

*Haley snaps into action. The music picks up a bit.*

HALEY: School?

JOYCE: Already notified of your absence.

HALEY: Home?

JOYCE: You fly to Las Vegas tonight. Number Twenty-Nine will give you your new passport. Number Eighty-Four will accompany you as your parent; do not discuss any aspect of the assignment with him or her; you'll find a car waiting at the airport, from which Eighty-Four will be ejected en route to the hotel.

HALEY: And what . . . will I use once I find him?

JOYCE: Bare knuckles. Fingernails; jaws.

And this.

*Music stops. The office dissolves.*


## Scene 4: Voicemail. Carver Speaking

*Carver leaves a voicemail for Morton.*

CARVER: Hey there. Me again. I like your outgoing message. It's very direct. Just wanted to let you know you're all set with the ticket. You have to change planes in Denver but that shouldn't be too bad. It's one of the nicer airports. Tell your mom. Alright.

*Pause.*

Hey there. Me again. I like your outgoing message. It's very direct. Just wanted to let you know you're all set with the ticket. You have to change planes in Denver but that shouldn't be too bad. It's one of the nicer airports. Tell your mom. Alright.

*Pause.*

Hey there. Me again. I like your outgoing message. I

*Morton exits.*


## Scene 5: Las Vegas

*Carver is on a date with Joyce. Joyce is a showgirl. Haley watches.*

JOYCE: For business?

CARVER: I do find myself here pretty regularly.

JOYCE: Can I ask, what do you do?

CARVER: Freelance.

JOYCE: That's nice. You can be your own man and make decisions. I know it gets very stressful though, if you're someone who needs to feel secure.

CARVER: Are you that kind of person?

JOYCE: Sometimes.

CARVER: Maybe you also like feeling insecure. Sometimes.

JOYCE: I used to do crazy things. When I first moved here I was out of control. I worked with snakes.

CARVER: I hate snakes.

JOYCE: They're not so bad. You just have to be firm.

CARVER: But you were out of control.

JOYCE: Not with the snakes. They focused me. That's what I mean.

CARVER: Ok, I see.

JOYCE: I was at a point where I needed something really violent like that. See? So that was just an indication, I'm using it as an example.

CARVER: I get you.

JOYCE: But then after a while the girl from the jaguar number left, she had a kid actually, and they asked me would I do that, and it was better exposure so I had to give up the snakes. But by that time I was more pulled together.

CARVER: Was there a real jaguar?

JOYCE: Good question. No, it was me, I was the jaguar. That was when Cats was really big. I was dressed up like a sexy cat.

*They envision it.*

Had a fight with the makeup artist, though. Whiskers.

CARVER: I never saw Cats.

JOYCE: No.

CARVER: I think I would have preferred your show.

JOYCE: Preferrrrrred.

*They both smile.*

CARVER: Did you have a tail?

JOYCE: Tails are funny. Do you like tails?

CARVER: Well…

JOYCE: It's a big thing, actually.

CARVER: Really.

JOYCE: Yeah. You didn't know that?

CARVER: I never thought about it.

JOYCE: Well, you should think about it. It makes sense, if you read…

*Beat.*

books.

CARVER: But I guess I do like tails. Yes.

JOYCE: Makes sense.

CARVER: Do jaguars have long skinny tails? Or fluffy. Or short.

JOYCE: What's your favorite?

CARVER: Long skinny.

JOYCE: Like a rat tail?

CARVER: No. Furry. Skinny but still furry.

JOYCE: You have all the answers.

CARVER: You're an inspiring presence.

JOYCE: Thank you.

CARVER: But.

*Pause.*

JOYCE: Oh. It was because—

CARVER: Not that I—

JOYCE: No. One of the Jungle Africans, he was from Reno, I won't mention his name, he and I had a stormy relationship.

CARVER: It was Jaguars and Africans?

JOYCE: Sure, it was . . .

*Beat.*

　　Oh.

CARVER: Because I believe jaguars are from South America.

JOYCE: Africans. Why did I think that?

CARVER: They could have been Olmecs. For instance.

JOYCE: Bones. Feathers.

CARVER: And things didn't go well?

JOYCE: Sometimes I think my brain is wearing out.

CARVER: You fought.

JOYCE: It's important. Isn't it? Something like that is important.

CARVER: And so you were offered another position and you took it.

JOYCE: What? Look. We can't always be available to others. We would like to be, and we work very hard to make it happen. Then when exhaustion kicks in, to the point of almost dead, we have to start making decisions. It's now only from the inside out that we can be justified. That's the structure that makes it possible to leave the place where we happen to be. Unlike clams.

CARVER: Makes sense to me.

JOYCE: Are you the same way?

CARVER: Very much.

JOYCE: But you have to come to it.

CARVER: Oh, you have to fight.

JOYCE: I just think it's the only way not to feel pain all the time.

CARVER: I agree, but. It seems to me that there's a danger there also.

JOYCE: Yeah?

CARVER: Maybe not for you. I mean,

*He indicates her body.*

That's a successful . . . that's success for sure.

I'd love to buy you something.

JOYCE: Let me think about what I want.

CARVER: No. Don't think about it. Let me think about it.

I could buy you anything. I feel like that right now.

JOYCE: Tell me.

CARVER: Oh man. Even just buying you another drink, I can feel how it would feel right now.

JOYCE: Funny.

CARVER: I can afford a lot. To buy a lot of stuff for a lot of women. That's the advantage of being the person I've become.

JOYCE: See that store?

CARVER: Yeah.

JOYCE: They have a display right inside, of bracelets.

CARVER: Yeah? Stop, stop!

*They sip their drinks.*

JOYCE: *(Going back to something he said earlier)* What's the danger?

CARVER: That you might wind up causing harm to those around you, without realizing it.

JOYCE: I'm glad you know what I mean.

## Scene 6: Morton's Room

*Haley is reading from the Internet on the Cube. Morton has fallen asleep. We can still hear the TV.*

HALEY: Vegas may be Sin City, but there are still plenty of things that the whole family can enjoy: magician Lance Burton at the Monte Carlo, Tournament of Kings dinner theater, the World's Largest Permanent Circus at Circus Circus, buffets, and hiking. Disney's The Lion King at Mandalay Bay is another good choice for children. The show features all of the lovable characters and songs from the hit animated movie. Stop and shop at the Forum Shops where the kids can enjoy the Festival Fountain. Want to sneak some education in with some fun? Then take them to see the Bodies the Exhibition, where your kids can check out all sorts of real-life bones and organs. For the adventurous preteens, they can experience the adrenaline rush with indoor cart racing at Pole Position Raceway. As long as they meet the height requirement, they're good to go.

*To Morton:*

You should—

*Morton is asleep. Haley transmits a message to him:*

We quieted down the dogs and hitched it, all the way from Goose Bay to Battle Harbour, see our breath ha we couldn't see nothing our eyeballs frozen over and it felt like. What the hell is that I said that's no cod as it comes up bump under the ice and we start sliding, that's some kinda mammal—

MORTON: *(Sleepily)* Shit, what time is it.

HALEY: *(Reading again)* Try the Shark Reef at Mandalay Bay or the gardens at the Flamingo with live Chilean flamingos, Mandarin ducks and koi. What's that?

MORTON: What?

HALEY: Koi.

MORTON: Goldfish.

HALEY: *(Reading again)* Youngsters will definitely get / a kick out—

MORTON: How are you still here?

HALEY: What if he's really weird?

MORTON: Bring my blade.

HALEY: On the plane? You would have to check it.

*Beat.*

And you're only going for a few days. You're gonna check baggage? Luggage? You know you have to pay for that now.

MORTON: How much?

HALEY: Like twenty-five bucks.

MORTON: (*Watching TV while he talks*) He's not taller than me. I'm taller now. He wears glasses. For reading, for reading contracts. He has a blade. He's a ladies' man. Uh, he has a wild and unprincipled smile. He can speak Serbo-Croatian. And Mexican Spanish. And the sign language of gangs, all the majors. He has accounts with, he has an account at. And you know, a lot of years on the

*Beat. Still watching.*

—or higher, so I'm not really too concerned.

HALEY: You think he's gonna get you a hooker?

MORTON: If he does...

*Pause. Morton settles back, drifting off to sleep.*

That'll be Sweeeet...

*Morton falls asleep. Haley watches TV for a little bit, sees that Morton isn't going to wake up, and goes home. She goes to sleep in exactly the same position as Morton. We hear Carver's voicemail.*

CARVER: Hey there. Me again.

*Morton and Haley shift, identically, in their sleep.*

Hey champ. Hey kangaroo.
Hey fuzzyhead. Hey little
Sleeper.

## Scene 7: Romantic Comedic

*The Cube glows bright. Joyce, no longer a showgirl, lies down asleep in the grass. We can hear birds chirping and other morning sounds. Light rises: pleasant outdoor country-side. Carver enters holding a coffee.*

CARVER: Morning. I hope you like white chocolate mocha.

> *Joyce stirs and sits up. Haley stirs and sits up, and holds out her hand for the coffee. Carver hands it to Joyce and sits beside her.*

JOYCE: It's my favorite, actually.

CARVER: I took a wild guess.

JOYCE: I'm usually too embarrassed to order it. It's so girly.

CARVER: You don't want to be girly?

JOYCE: No!

CARVER: Could've fooled me last night.

JOYCE: Last night?

> *She rubs her head.*

    Oh god.

CARVER: The tow truck's on its way.

JOYCE: What happened last night, exactly?

CARVER: You wowed a room full of locals with your soul-nourishing rendition of Duran Duran.

HALEY: Ugh.

JOYCE: Well . . . thanks.

> *Joyce takes a sip of coffee and puts the cup down. During the next couple of lines, Haley sneaks up and grabs the coffee, then settles in with it to watch the scene.*

CARVER: This is where I pull out a pack of American Spirits and enjoy a morning smoke with my coffee. Only I quit five years ago.

JOYCE: I'm glad you quit.

CARVER: I figured it was time to stop letting other guys decide.

JOYCE: So it was like a . . . macho thing?

CARVER: Yeah, I guess it was.

*All three laugh.*

JOYCE: A real macho guy who excels at karaoke!

CARVER: Hey, you were the one singing. I was just cheering from the stands.

JOYCE: I seem to recall someone doing a pretty outrageous Simon Le Bon impression.

*Haley shakes her head in amused disgust.*

CARVER: I thought you said you didn't remember!

    (*To Haley*) And how do you know who Simon Le Bon is?

HALEY: I'm fifteen, Carver, I'm not a moron.

CARVER: (*To Joyce*) The plumber should be here soon.

JOYCE: Oh, for the—

CARVER: Right.

JOYCE: Right.

CARVER: For a little girl you sure do a lot of damage.

JOYCE: I guess I—

CARVER: Don't tell me: you come from a broken home.

HALEY: *(Incredulous)* No.

CARVER: Raised by wolves?

JOYCE: No. My parents are extremely human.

*Beat.*

    They're great.

HALEY: We'd go on picnics.

CARVER: Well then you . . . are a mystery.

JOYCE: I'm / a mystery?

HALEY: I'm a mystery?

*Playfully, Joyce gets closer to Carver. Haley watches intently.*

JOYCE: You're the one everyone's dying to meet, lying awake nights wondering what color your eyes will be, what your voice sounds like, whether you ever smile, whether you give good hugs, or any hugs...

*Carver hugs Joyce. A long hug.*

*Meanwhile Morton wakes up in his room. He takes a suitcase and goes to the airport. Then he's in the airport. Haley sees Morton go.*

*Carver and Joyce hold each other tenderly.*

CARVER: I think you might be the sweetest person I've ever come across.

JOYCE: Really?

CARVER: Then again, the circles I move in...

*Joyce hits Carver, not hard. He grabs her hand and holds it.*

*Haley gets up and leaves the scene, which continues without her. She goes into Morton's room, tapping the Cube as she passes. Duran Duran's "Hungry Like the Wolf" comes on. She picks up the Guitar Hero guitar and plays.*

Listen, Joyce, I don't know how to say this. For some reason I guess I never thought I'd have to.

I always used to tell myself that I just wasn't that kind of guy. That I was ... "strong."

*Haley sings along with the music.*

HALEY: Do-do-do do-do-do do-do-do do-do-do, do do do

CARVER: But there's something about you that makes me feel different, like a different person, someone who could take it on, say: yes, I can take it on. I will. I want to take care of you, Joyce. Not just buy you a nice bracelet or pay for your cab, I've done those things, it's not what I'm talking about.

JOYCE: What are you talking about?

HALEY: *(Singing along)* In touch with the ground, I'm on the hunt I'm after you

CARVER: I want your happiness, and your health, and your—your everything to be my responsibility.

HALEY: *(Singing along)* And I'm hungry like the wooolf

CARVER: If there's a second in the day when you're not smiling, I want to be the one whose fault it is. Who has to work the earth and manipulate the sky to make you smile again.

*Morton appears at the airport. In the following, Joyce and Carver are talking only to each other, as are Morton and Haley.*

MORTON: Hey.

JOYCE: Yeah?

CARVER: Yeah.

MORTON: Hey. It's Morton.

JOYCE: Ok.

CARVER: Ok?

MORTON: I got you something from the airport.

*Haley has some trouble concentrating on the game.*

JOYCE: Ok. Yeah.

HALEY: Yeah?

*Carver tickles Joyce. Joyce giggles and they look into each other's eyes and they both giggle.*

MORTON: It's a Chapstick that says Las Vegas on it. It's Apple Martini flavor.

*Carver and Joyce begin to dance.*

HALEY: Do-do-do do-do-do do-do-do do-do-do, do do do

MORTON: Cher's playing here this weekend. And also Green Day. So it says "Green Day. Sold Out." Thought maybe you'd think that's funny.

HALEY: Ha

MORTON: OH SHIT.

*The music stops. Everyone turns to look at Morton.*

There's my dad.

*Carver, Joyce, and Morton exit. Haley is alone onstage.*

*Haley grows up.*

# Part Two

## Scene 8: Haley is 25. She Goes to Work. She Works for Joyce.

JOYCE: Have you seen...?

HALEY: Mmm.

JOYCE: No. Look, uh, can you come here for a minute? I want to explain to you a series of things that might be involved.

HALEY: Maybe I'll write—

JOYCE: Yeah. No, I think it's important you keep it in your head, that you be able to. So just.

HALEY: Yeah.

JOYCE: What I'm looking for is ... doesn't matter because, ok. Haley. It's possible that I might have to go away for a few days. Out of town.

HALEY: Oh, is everything ok?

JOYCE: Uh, well...?

HALEY: It's not—

JOYCE: No, that's all right, it's an appropriate question, I am grateful, but yeah, I think everything is ok.

HALEY: Good.

JOYCE: Listen though, let's not get sidetracked. The point is that we need to stay on the ball. This is the climax of the quarter that we're approaching.

HALEY: Right.

JOYCE: So it's important that we check in.

*Haley nods. Joyce nods. They nod slowly and look at each other.*

Do you think...?

HALEY: I'm ... ready to stay on the ball, yeah. I'm counting on moving into high, high-density activity.

JOYCE: I just want to be sure. That.

*The phone rings. Joyce expects Haley to answer it. Haley does.*

HALEY: Aster House. Hi George, yeah we were just gonna give you a call.

*Haley mouths "excuse me" to Joyce and moves aside to take this business call. Joyce gets out an improbable duffel bag and opens it. She looks through it, furtively, muttering to herself.*

JOYCE: Yes, two, jackalope...

HALEY: *(Loudly, on the phone)* No. George, let me back up, I don't want you to have that impression because that's really not at all what's likely at this point.

*Joyce hurriedly puts the bag away. Stands for a moment.*

JOYCE: Thank you, I'd just love it.

*Haley is finished with the call.*

How's George?

HALEY: Obstreperous. But / I think I—

JOYCE: I'm sure.

HALEY: He did want—

JOYCE: Great. That shouldn't be a problem.

HALEY: No.

JOYCE: So.

HALEY: "As you were saying."

JOYCE: No, I don't wanna be theatrical about it. The point is just that I need you to ... focus.

Pay attention.

Not to me right now. / I mean

HALEY: Oh.

JOYCE: Right. These next few days: a little extra attention if you can. I'm not maligning your, please don't think that I'm maligning, see, this is a risk you run when you initiate this kind of conversation and I've lost employees before through this particular misunderstanding so it's important to me that you understand your work's been fully ...

*Pause.*

HALEY: Satisfactory?

JOYCE: There's nothing negative about what I'm saying. Let's be clear. Nothing negative. I just want to encourage you, especially in my absence if that should turn out to be the case, even though it would only be for a few days, ok?

HALEY: Encourage me...

JOYCE: This isn't about productivity, so I'm glad to hear you're, what? Stepping it up? But, really I'm not trivializing that. But, what I'm talking about is refinement, of, perception.

HALEY: Refinement.

JOYCE: Perception.

HALEY: I see.

*The phone rings again. Haley answers.*

Aster House. Who's calling please? Let me see if she's available.

*To JOYCE:*

Greg from Enter?

*Joyce looks at Haley. Haley looks at Joyce. Pause.*

I'm so sorry Greg, she's in a meeting right now. Would you like her voice-mail? Thank you.

*Haley hangs up.*

JOYCE: Ok.

*They exit in opposite directions.*

## Scene 9. Haley and Martin's Apartment

*Martin is alone in the apartment he shares with Haley.*

MARTIN: Dear Sir or Madam. I'd like to identify myself as a candidate for this position. Here I am. Sincerely, Martin.

To Whom it May Concern, hello. Let me tell you.

I believe that these experiences, combined with my strong background in writing and my keen interest in artistic experimentation, make me a good candidate for the Program Manager position.

Although I am not a dancer myself

Attached.

My excellences are referent.

*Pause.*

We quieted down the dogs, a great big bird, a cor...
A corp...
A cormorant. Six of them. Sitting there. Wings folded. Wings extended.
Uh—
Yeeah—

*Makes a movement as if to grab something in his pocket. Stops: failure.*

Mm.
Crap.

*Beat.*

Dear Martin.
Crap. What are we, babies?

*Haley enters, home from work.*

We should move to Newfoundland.

HALEY: What's there?

MARTIN: Snow. And then water.

HALEY: Oh right, I remember. Were you watching / that again?

MARTIN: No I was reading in the / news.

HALEY: I wouldn't mind watching that again, it was so peaceful.

MARTIN: Maybe what we'll do is I'll go first and set up a homestead.

HALEY: Are there incentives?

MARTIN: What?

HALEY: Incentives from . . . or what was the news?

MARTIN: No.

HALEY: Just more of those girls with the round—

MARTIN: I guess.

HALEY: Well sure, let's do some research.

MARTIN: I already have.

HALEY: How'd it go today?

MARTIN: What?

HALEY: The project.

*Pause.*

MARTIN: What project?

HALEY: Sorry, sorry for asking.

MARTIN: How was work?

HALEY: Joyce is concerned about something.

MARTIN: Joyce...

HALEY: My boss?

MARTIN: It's one of those names that / sounds like other names.

HALEY: She's concerned about my perception. I thought my perception was good.

MARTIN: Of...?

HALEY: No. She meant, she thinks, or she's afraid that I might miss something or be missing something. —Can I turn that down? —What is it that she thinks I don't notice?

MARTIN: Ask her.

HALEY: She's my, and she's been kind of distracted or aggrieved, it's not just about me, there's something.

MARTIN: Sorry. I'm sure it'll become clear.

HALEY: Why?

MARTIN: Because there aren't really any secrets. Mysteries.

HALEY: Oh.


## Scene 10. Haley and Martin in Bed

*It is the middle of the night. Martin is asleep. The Cube glows.*

HALEY: Martin.

Martin.

MARTIN: Mmf.

HALEY: Can you turn it off?

Will you turn it off please, I can't reach.

*The Cube's light goes out. Haley goes to sleep. Darkness.*

MARTIN: We quieted down the dogs and hitched it, all the way from Goose Bay to Battle Harbour, see our breath ha we couldn't see nothing our eyeballs frozen over and it felt like. What the hell is that I said that's no cod as it comes up bump under the ice and we start sliding, that's some kinda mammal and you've got your mind on blueberries and partridgeberries and bakeapples. About mid-morning we pass by a family of girls driving their pack back from town, all in the same hats. Hope it stays clear for them I said. It can be brutal. It can be brutal out here but it's always fair. After a while the land and the sky is empty again and we keep on.

*Silence.*

Haley?

*Long silence.*

It's not true because
I have a secret.
Always.

*Lights come up. Haley is staring at Martin. Martin is asleep. Pause. An alarm goes off.*

HALEY: Ugh dreamt I messed everything up and I came home and wanted to tell you but you said that part of your life was over and you wouldn't talk about it. Could we do something about the TV?

MARTIN: I'll look into it.

HALEY: Thanks.

*She leaves for work. After Haley exits, Martin exits.*

## Scene 11: The Office

*Joyce is alone in the office. Practicing.*

JOYCE: No, Carver, and here's why not. I would never, look at me sweetheart, I would NEVER betray you. You're everything to me. —No no, shit, no, what are you, what are you doing with that heavy thing? AAAAHfuck.

It's my life and I worked hard for it and I'm not gonna

And I'll do whatever it takes to stay to keep

To get you to trust me, trust me. Look, I've got a lot to lose, it means a lot to me, this business, maybe you can't see that maybe to you it looks like captivity, it's not a Swiss bank account and an unlimited supply of freedom and cummy freedom and oozy floozy watusi in every joint from here to fucking fucking help. —Because I'll do it if you take one more step. Think about the kind of thing this is, it's the kind where, the contemporary vision where I might totally do it and not even on a downbeat I'll do it on a while you're talking or while I'm, yeah there's no reason to hold back, I've got nothing

to lose, and that's because of you because look at me, you've shriveled my
breasts, I can only eat taffy, my hair is gone, I just sit there watching . . .

Yeah I've got nothing, just get it over with you ravishing slugheaded man-
dril, just right between the goddamn eyes.

Not ravishing, not ravishing.

Haley?

*Haley enters.*

HALEY: Did you want me in early?
JOYCE: No.

*Long Pause.*

HALEY: Are...?
　　　Is there anything I can . . .
　　　dooo?
JOYCE: Yah.
　　　Go out and come in again and don't make any sound. No sound, don't even
　　　breathe, he doesn't.
HALEY: Um.
JOYCE: I wanna see when I notice. If I notice if I'm facing this way. I just wanna see
　　　how susceptible I might be. If I'm say reading. Pass me that. If I'm standing
　　　here reading this...

*She stands reading. Haley hesitates, then exits. Pause. Haley enters, slowly, si-
lently.*

I don't see you.

*Haley stops, confused.*

I said I don't see you, keep coming.

*Haley approaches. Joyce pretends to whip out a gun and turn it on Haley.*

BANG!

HALEY: JESUS!

JOYCE: Boom.

HALEY: H—

JOYCE: Safety though. Have to practice.

*Joyce puts the "gun" away.*

HALEY: Th, th, gk...

JOYCE: Oh. I see, yah. Sorry, I should have mentioned. Although I don't know what else you thought would happen. And you're so pliable all the time, so eager to please, you give the impression people can do whatever they want to you. It's the same old schoolyard logic. Same old boys' bathroom. Dig?

HALEY: Yeah. Um.

JOYCE: Thank you. You're very popular around here, Haley.

Never let it be said

not.

## Scene 12: A Diner

*Martin is sitting alone in a booth at the diner, working on his project. The Cube is his table. Carver sits at the counter.*

CARVER: Just coffee. Wait. You know what? Sandwich.

Ah... liverwurst, you have that? No onions no.

*The waitress leaves.*

Not gonna. Eat it, not gonna "take it home." Haha.

MARTIN: Coke. Thanks a lot.

*Martin works on his project. Carver watches him. This goes on for a while. Carver gets his food. Martin, barely audible:*

One; two; jackalope...

CARVER: *(Annoyed)* Ahh.

*Martin looks at Carver for the first time. Carver nods, small smile. Martin looks away.*

They put onions on it.

*Martin doesn't look at him.*

It's like that thing with elephants. Never should have said the word. You want it? I'm not gonna.

MARTIN: [No] Thanks.

CARVER: Liverwurst.

MARTIN: That's disgusting to me.

CARVER: Hed.

I'm the one.

What are you working on over there?

*Martin signals for the check.*

No.

*Carver comes over to Martin's booth and sits.*

MARTIN: *(To waitress)* Can I get the check?

CARVER: *(To waitress)* It's on me. Put it on mine.

MARTIN: No, I'm.

CARVER: Morton.

MARTIN: Uh. No.

CARVER: What? —Listen.

MARTIN: I'm not, that's.

CARVER: Listen. Don't you:

*Gestures over his own face. Martin doesn't answer.*

Or how about this how about this how about this blah blah voice how about. Remembering the sound of this and it's coming back right, the timbre, the specifics?

MARTIN: No. You're I think taking me for someone.

CARVER: I said I'm the guy.

MARTIN: I know.

I don't know what you meant when you said that.

Excuse me.

*Martin rises. Carver rises. Martin starts breathing heavily. They stand for a while.*
*Martin stops breathing heavily. They sit again.*

CARVER: Ok?

*Martin nods. To waitress:*

Another coke please. And a slice of pie. No ice cream. WAIT! What did I ask for. Right. Y—right.

*To Martin:*

If she brings it and it has the ice cream on it, we'll push it off onto my saucer right away, and it'll just be a little bit of white film on the top crust. That's ok, right?

MARTIN: Yeah.

CARVER: Want no onions, keep the yap shut.

MARTIN: "No 'no' in the unconscious." That's what they say.

CARVER: They haven't seen mine.

MARTIN: It's not really a project, it's more of an interest that I'm exploring to see whether I might want it to become a project later on.

CARVER: Right.

MARTIN: I don't really talk about it with anyone.

CARVER: Good idea.

MARTIN: Yeah, exactly, and then you feel pressures and people start asking. You generate all this commentary and then you can't find what it was actually gonna be—

CARVER: What was drawing you—

MARTIN: It just becomes another—

CARVER: Yup. Yup.

MARTIN: Mm but I think though, I'll just say I think it's. Gonna.

CARVER: I don't doubt it.

*Pause. They sit.*

Couple things.

MARTIN: Yeah.

CARVER: One.

I understand that you feel things are basically going well. That there's not a lot that's out of your reach. Nothing you might really want that you couldn't, if you put it to it, have. Or do. I'm supposing it'd be doing more than having.

*Martin shrugs.*

But there's not a lack, it doesn't feel like poverty.

MARTIN: No.

CARVER: No. That's absolutely reasonable.

MARTIN: Haley has a pretty good job—

CARVER: HAKK

MARTIN: Yeah.

What?

CARVER: Time enough, excuse me, dust from the desert.

MARTIN: Desert?

CARVER: That's right. Please.

MARTIN: That Haley my girlfriend has a pretty good job, and I'm getting unemployment. So.

CARVER: *(As if not sure which point to address first)* Mhm.

What I want to emphasize is that this point of view has a lot to do with your frame of reference. I'd like you to bear that in mind.

Two.

By contrast. I'd like to show you some pictures.

*Carver taps the Cube and an image appears. The photo and all those that follow are very impressive.*

MARTIN: Your house?

CARVER: One of.

*No one will know, but the next photo is an expensive car. Then: a beautiful pedigreed dog.*

MARTIN: Ohh.

CARVER: That's Theodor. Ever watch the Eukanuba Championship?

MARTIN: Sometimes. Was he—?

CARVER: That's right.

MARTIN: Wow.

CARVER: If anyone tried to hurt you.

MARTIN: He'd rip out their throat?

*The next picture is a private jet. Then a tropical landscape. Then a very fancy high-rollers-only room at a casino. Joyce appears in the photo in her showgirl costume, not in the center and not looking at the camera.*

Who's that?

CARVER: Yeah. One minute.

*Then a Newfoundland landscape.*

You know where this is?

MARTIN: Newfoundland?

CARVER: It's completely empty.

*Now onstage we also see Haley and Joyce in the office.*

HALEY: I have a strategy I've been pioneering. When I'm . . . nervous or under the weather.

Well I, assuming I know what's bothering me, I.

*Long pause.*

JOYCE: *(Referring to something business-related)* Can you deal with this today?

HALEY: Sure.

JOYCE: I'm just a little...

Swamped.

HALEY: Joyce—

*Joyce exits fast. Martin and Carver in the diner, looking through the photographs.*

CARVER: Now ask me again.

MARTIN: Oh. Who's that.

CARVER: 't's Joyce.

*Martin looks across the stage at Haley.*

MARTIN: Uh-huh.

*Looks back at Carver.*

Uh-huh.

Um—

CARVER: Don't! It's all right to sit. And think about it.

*The pie arrives. Martin sighs.*

What is that? No, that's off-putting, he doesn't want that.

MARTIN: It's ok.

CARVER: No, I didn't say ANYthing about whipped cream, I said no ICE cream, I said NOTHING, did you Morton?

MARTIN: Martin.

CARVER: Thank you.

MARTIN: *(Quietly)* And could you—

CARVER: Excuse me! —Go ahead.

MARTIN: And could you warm it up please. Thanks.

CARVER: Good idea.

MARTIN: You'll have some, right?

CARVER: Will you?

Have some?

*The office. Joyce reenters.*

JOYCE: Think I'd gone?

HALEY: Hmm?

JOYCE: Did you, did you think I'd hide, mm, did you think I had hide, whoah. Did ...you...think...I...had...high...tailed it?

HALEY: I thought you maybe weren't feeling well.

JOYCE: Can you stay late?

HALEY: Sure.

JOYCE: I'll give you a big fat bonus.

HALEY: That's ok, I / can stay

JOYCE: Til three?

HALEY: What? A.M.?

JOYCE: That's when I think it's gonna start to get light, around three. Too late?

HALEY: It might be, I just / had some things I—

JOYCE: Big bonus? No? Checkers? We can play checkers. / Chinese checkers.

HALEY: It's an Asian client, or?

JOYCE: What no. Yeah. Maybe something like that. No, don't listen to me.

HALEY: I think it stays dark much later.

JOYCE: No. The almanac.

HALEY: But actually—

JOYCE: You don't want to stay. That's fine. There's a limit to what I can ... demand. I don't want to be rapacious.

HALEY: Well, what did you need me to do? Maybe I can start on it now.

JOYCE: Do you think of me as rapacious? As a rapist essentially?

HALEY: No.

JOYCE: Here's the thing. I didn't watch where I was going. I didn't ... look both ways.

HALEY: With—?

JOYCE: With, with heedless disregard is what with. For the future. Because I thought, what is that? Compared to this, this. And so.

HALEY: You
The company?

JOYCE: I think that the more you do not know, the more. Yah.

HALEY: So the
Bureau? Or—

JOYCE: No. All right, let me lay it out. If you don't hear from me. Within a reasonable time frame. Well: probably I'm dead. But there's another possibility and that's where you do hear from me and I want to enlist your support. Could I have that?

Baby?

HALEY: Yeah of course

JOYCE: There's somewhere I might be. There's somewhere I might be and I might let you know.

HALEY: Where?

JOYCE: I'll let you know. Ok? Listen. Keep:

*Circle hand gesture to indicate the office.*

> You can do it I'm happy
> With your performance, you can
> Do it. You'll know.

*Joyce pulls out her duffel bag and exits: really exits.*

*Haley taps the Cube and music starts to play.*

*Haley sings karaoke to "I Would" by Jane's Addiction.*

*The song ends.*


## Scene 13: Carver's Fancy Apartment

*Haley, Martin, and Carver are having drinks in Carver's apartment. Carver enters with a drink for Haley.*

CARVER: White chocolatini.

*Haley takes the drink. She is the only one who has one. She sips it.*

HALEY: Yum.

MARTIN: Carver's been to Newfoundland.

HALEY: Oh really?

CARVER: Beautiful.

HALEY: Really, I bet.

MARTIN: He has a sss— *(suddenly not sure if this is true)* —table?

HALEY: A what?

CARVER & MARTIN: Stable.

HALEY: Of . . . animals?

MARTIN: No, of people.

HALEY: I don't know what that means.

MARTIN: Of animals, of course.

CARVER: Animals.

HALEY: *(Nodding)* Um.

Do you mind if I smoke?

*Carver holds out a lighter.*

That's pretty.

MARTIN: Yeah, it's cool, it reminds me of like, uh, something I was reading.

*Carver lights Haley's cigarette.*

HALEY: Thank you.

MARTIN: Damn.

*Carver offers the lighter to Martin.*

CARVER: Keep it.

HALEY & MARTIN: No!

CARVER: Jog your memory. Later. When you're at your ease.

MARTIN: That's OK. Really.

*But he takes it.*

HALEY: Very n—

*She coughs.*

Very nice of you.

MARTIN: Yeah, why're you smoking?

HALEY: "Stress."

*All laugh loudly.*

CARVER: Don't you want to know what kind of animals?

HALEY: Oh right. There's different kinds.

MARTIN: Reindeer. Right?

HALEY: Right, reindeer! Like the girls with the round—
 In this documentary we like.

CARVER: Oh, I know. I know them.

MARTIN: They seem nice.

CARVER: They're nice.

HALEY: That's right? Reindeer?

CARVER: Among other things.

HALEY: But it's so cold. Isn't it?

CARVER: We have some technology for that.

HALEY: So?
 What other...

*Long silence.*

CARVER: How's everyone for drinks?

HALEY & MARTIN: Good.

CARVER: It's been a while.

HALEY: Since—

CARVER: Since I played host. I usually entertain abroad.

HALEY: Haha

CARVER: Oh, silly, yes, right.

HALEY: You meant, out in the world.

CARVER: Exactly.

HALEY: It's a really lovely
 Apartment.

CARVER: Thank you. It lacks something I think, that lived-in quality, I'm hardly
 ever here.

MARTIN: But I think that's great. Our place is so cluttered, I always think we
 should just get rid of everything.

HALEY: You could sublet it.

CARVER: That's true.

HALEY: If what you want is—

CARVER: That's not really what I want.

MARTIN: And camp out under the windows.

HALEY: What do you think it is? That you want?

MARTIN: Haley.

HALEY: Yeah?

CARVER: Shut up Morton. Haley. You're turned on?

HALEY: What?

CARVER: I answered your question with a question.

HALEY: Huh.

MARTIN: Wum.

HALEY: Aaaah. This has been the weirdest.

CARVER: I know.

HALEY: My boss...

MARTIN: Joyce?

CARVER: (Hak.)

HALEY: Oh, it's been so.

CARVER: Don't worry about it.

HALEY: I am worried though. I am.

CARVER: You just think you are. But it's impossible, because I put an anti-anxiety medicament in your drink.

MARTIN: Haha.

CARVER: I did!

HALEY: Really?

    Awesome.

CARVER: I'm the guy.

MARTIN: Yeah, wait.

HALEY: Why do you keep calling him—

MARTIN: Wait.

HALEY: I did have a—

CARVER: I know.

HALEY: You do?

CARVER: I know so much. I know...

What I know...

It's staggering and wild, how big.

How massive what I know.

MARTIN: I think that maybe it's getting to be the time when we're ready to leave, is that cool Haley?

HALEY: You're leaving?

MARTIN: Aren't you tired? You've been working so much. With Joyce gone.

*That name makes Carver gag a little again.*

HALEY: I'm ok. I think I might pass out.

MARTIN: Well that's what let's go.

CARVER: You won't pass out. What's the problem, Morton?

MARTIN: There's no problem. I'm tired, I thought— *(To Haley)* thought you'd be tired.

CARVER: Haley's having a great time. I put a stimulant in her drink.

HALEY: Oh God.

CARVER: You're tired, so why don't you sack out in there. While I mount your girlfriend.

HALEY: Oh God.

CARVER: While I / fuck this young woman who still would not be the youngest woman I've fucked this month, not by a long shot, not by a decade, much less the most attractive—

MARTIN: I don't understand what you're doing, this isn't what we talked about, is it? I didn't understand, I actually still don't understand why this needs to be part of the plan or actually what the plan is anymore since I guess I was confused actually the whole time—

CARVER: I'm just kidding.

HALEY: Hey!

What are the other animals?

*This part of the scene ends.*

*The next part of the scene is still in Carver's apartment, a while later that evening. Martin is tied up in the next room. Haley is woozy.*

CARVER: What else did she say?

HALEY: It was really hard to tell.

CARVER: How can you get in touch with her?

HALEY: I can't.

CARVER: She just left you . . . unequivocally . . . in charge. Forever.

HALEY: She said she would contact me.

CARVER: When?

HALEY: I don't know. She had a gun.

CARVER: What? So what, I have fifty guns.

HALEY: Fifty. You're fifty.

   She said what she was telling me was not what I thought she was telling me.

CARVER: Which was?

HALEY: Uh.

CARVER: What did you think, that wasn't what it was?

HALEY: I thought she was saying about the business, that it was involved in shady deals. That she was a, maybe a white-collar. . .
   Enthusiast.

CARVER: She never mentioned a place? In
   Space?

HALEY: I won't be in charge forever. Even if she never does, I won't stay there for the rest of my life. There's other things I wanna do. For instance. Congress.

*Pause.*

   She gave me. . .

*Pause.*

   What pedal?

*A few days pass. Finally Carver is talking on the phone and Haley is watching a cooking show on the Cube.*

CARVER: Da. Ponudi ih jeftino seljacima. Za polovinu. Dobicemo njihovo poverenje. To je investicija, ne gubitak. U redu?

[Yes, offer them to the farming population at a cut rate. Half price. That will make them trust us. It's an investment, not a loss. Ok?]

*The Cube beeps in a new way. Haley jumps up, sees that Carver has seen her reaction, and sits back down. Carver goes to the Cube. He stares at it. He gets the message. He walks over to Haley.*

HALEY: She's not there now, she said.

CARVER: Get up, you're coming.

HALEY: Why?

CARVER: Negotiation.

HALEY: Where?

CARVER: It'll be fun.

HALEY: Newfoundland?

*Martin, in the other room, is aggrieved. Carver puts out his hand to Haley. She reaches up and takes it. He pulls her to her feet.*

Las Vegas?

*Carver and Haley exit. They take an airplane trip. Martin stays behind.*


## Scene 14: Las Vegas/Newfoundland

*The airport: Arrivals. Someone in a big black overcoat enters. She holds up a sign like a limo driver. It says "Carver." Of course this person is Joyce in disguise. Carver enters and identifies himself to the disguised Joyce, without recognizing her. She nods and makes an "after you" gesture.*

CARVER: Huh?

*Joyce repeats the gesture.*

Hang on. Just a minute, my young wife is in the ladies room.

*No visible response from Joyce. Then she turns her head to look for Haley.*

You know the address?

*No response.*

I said.

*Joyce turns back to face him. They look at each other for a while.*

Have plans for tonight?

*Joyce makes the comic gesture of slapping her thigh.*

Wha?

*They look at each other. Then Haley enters. Sees Joyce and recognizes her. Looks at Carver and sees that he does not recognize Joyce. Carver and Joyce look at her.*

HALEY: There's a...
     Ok.

*Carver leads the way.*

CARVER: Ok.

*All three exit.*

*Martin alone, still tied up in Carver's apartment.*

MARTIN: This is a love song.

*Pause.*

It's an experience I had.

*Pause.*

Acknowledgment. I'm gonna talk about my family now and things that I wanted. First of all. A firm fucking hand. Some guidance. Woulda been.

Also, uh, hope.

Understand it! You!

*Pause.*

I had a dream I messed everything up. And I wanted to talk to you about it but you said that since you were dead, that conversation could not be a priority. So I was crying.

In the dream, obviously.

*Pause.*

GET ME OUT!

*Haley, and Carver are in the limo that Joyce is driving. All are silent for a while.*

CARVER: *(To Haley)* You could amuse yourself by noticing all this and try to decide if it's beautiful. You know almost anything can do that. Fill that need.

*He gets a call.*

YAH.

*Haley turns and looks at him. He talks on the phone.*

Díle que no. No, lo que no necesito no compro.

Well if he's gonna drop everything...

*Haley leans forward toward Joyce. Joyce looks at her once, furtively, then back at the road.*

Oh she's what you'd call canny. Under no circumstances would I deny that or minimize that. The risk involved is involved. Because I need her—
JOYCE: *(Softly)* Alive.
CARVER: Exactly.

*The phone call is over.*

PUMPkin.

*Haley is startled.*

HALEY: Yeah.
CARVER: How ya feelin?

HALEY: I'm a little dehydrated.

CARVER: Well you're in the desert.

HALEY: Is it sand? Or snow?

CARVER: Get a load
of you.

HALEY: What is it that you need from Joyce?

CARVER: Something she has.

HALEY: How do you know she has it?

CARVER: It's mine.

HALEY: Is it a / substance?

CARVER: It's my heart.
And I can smell it.

*Pause. Haley leans forward to talk to Joyce.*

HALEY: Let's get out of here.

JOYCE: Since when?

HALEY: Let's go to your house.
I never visited you at your house.

JOYCE: It's a shithole.

HALEY: Well—

JOYCE: I can never bring anyone there.

HALEY: Isn't there something you could show me? You could show me around the
. . . piles?

JOYCE: I don't get it.

HALEY: I just think it's a shame.

JOYCE: You think it's a shame?

HALEY: What do you want? What do you want?

JOYCE: Shh!

*Joyce screeches the car to a halt.*

CARVER: Are we here?

*Carver, Joyce, and Haley get up.*

*Joyce takes off her coat to reveal the showgirl costume, but with pieces of winter wear incorporated.*

*There is the sound of whistling wind, desert or tundra. A lull.*

JOYCE: And?

CARVER: It's the good old dynamic.

JOYCE: Just...

CARVER: No. This is what I'm thinking about. When I'm out there. Living life. I think about being back here. With you.

JOYCE: I know what you think about.

CARVER: You don't, Joyce.

JOYCE: Well.

You don't know that about me.

CARVER: Well, I will.

JOYCE: No.

CARVER: Wanna hear what I have planned?

JOYCE: Carver—

CARVER: BRAIN torture.

JOYCE: Carver, do you think I'm an idiot? I took you here on purpose. We're on my turf now. This is the seat of my powers.

CARVER: Oh.

No.

Hmm.

HALEY: WHAT POWERS?

JOYCE: Don't interrupt, honey.

CARVER: What about her?

JOYCE: What.

CARVER: You wouldn't want to put her in danger.

JOYCE: Wouldn't be the first time.

CARVER: What kind of human being are you?

HALEY: Back off!

CARVER: *(Still to Joyce)* She's crazy about us!

HALEY: What?

JOYCE: Haley, get back in the car.

HALEY: Why?

JOYCE: Because everything is going to get destroyed.

HALEY: What? What will be destroyed?

CARVER: Everything.

HALEY: Even you?

CARVER: Especially me.

HALEY: But. I thought you can't die in / your—

CARVER: Who said anything about dreams?

*Martin yells from wherever he is:*

MARTIN: I MESSED EVERYTHING UP AND I WANT TO DISCUSS IT PLEASE

CARVER: Listen, everything—

JOYCE: Look at me.

*Carver and Haley look at her.*

MARTIN: EXCUSE ME

JOYCE: Everything is basically the same.

MARTIN: NOT EXCUSE I MEAN UH FORGIVE

CARVER: You see what this is the victory of.

JOYCE: Get back in the car.

HALEY: What good will that do?

CARVER: *(To Haley)* Later on I'll show you some things and you'll see why there's the thrill.

HALEY: All right...

*She backs away. Joyce and Carver square off.*

CARVER: Huh.

JOYCE: Hah.

CARVER: Nng.

JOYCE: Tt.

CARVER: When you were born I was on the road and I received a telegram in the language of our ancestors.

Can you try to imagine, can you try the walls of the van, fuzzy beige, totally indifferent to the crisis of my desire for you, which is unlike anything. Think about the scale, can you think about the scale of that problem. Can you imagine my objection. The underground warrens, the hives of what you then fomented. And as you grew

As you grew I saw even less, that means less than nothing, I knew even less, a negative number, caroming in blindness, a joke at my own expense, the networks, the fisheries of my lo— of my longing. And I'd go, what if we take a walk to watch the boats? And one time the tall ships and? My political questions and hatred and sense for unease that had won me fame or praise: all now a scaffold, a makeshift strewn willy-nilly, a tentscape, a 'fuge. My collection of record albums sat stock still, obsolescing. They're all right there on the shelves in puddles because glass is a liquid in fact, I mean in time.

This is actually kind of important, little baby, I screamed, and there was no upshot. At this point you're three feet, you're four feet tall and mute as a panda. I carry your hot pink pack up the hill in my hand. My mind is busy with plans for escaping you. I will never be finished, I'll always be making the plans, if you look at me once I'll have to start over, my plans are that...

Devastated

Look

I'm saying it look, you look at the thing in the shrubs, the creature, is this, is this

I will get you one of our own I will get you I promise

*Pause.*

JOYCE: Tt.
CARVER: Kk.
JOYCE: Boy Jesus what a stand-up type.

CARVER: No.

JOYCE: What a Lewis and Clark, what a friend to the dragons. What an architect! And here I was painting my toenails and obeying various … suggestions and never dreaming I had my own bank account.

When you were born I was flat out in hiding, out cold, just wasted when the call came in to wherever that was that I wasn't. You there at the other end of the line. In those days you had to ring up through the operator and you can imagine how that went. Hello? Yeah? No? 'Bye now. Like that, endlessly. Until the Muppets came on and taught you something else. Man I was a wreck in those days, but I had a terrible, demonic glamor. I had a sheen. I was Jewish as fuck. In fact I applied for asylum. I did. Feature? Because what I fe—

What I

God damn it I'd do anything so you would. Cmere take my cocoa and get under my cape. I want to think about something besides the future. The future can choke, it's where you leave me, covered in buttons of your own devising. That's what I whispered to you, fuck whispered, crooned. And our terror prevented nothing

But!

CARVER: Wait.

JOYCE: But!

You can't make me into this thing and expect to get away. And when you do get away, you can't expect to find your way back. And when you do get back, and you look at my face, it won't have anything to do with my face. I'm just saying. You won't understand. And when you understand, and you look around, what you'll see

Is that there's no other side. That the moon is flat.

*The whole theater, including the audience, is suddenly lit up.*

It's already showing us everything.

CARVER: I'm the one
    who knows that.

JOYCE: Yeah.

I'm that one.

*Carver and Joyce are both exhausted. They collapse.*

MARTIN: Haley.

*Haley looks at Martin.*

I thought about what I wanted to say.

*Haley thinks: maybe this will fix everything.*

What I would say to him.

*Nope.*

*Lights down on the audience and Martin.*

*Haley sits with the collapsed Carver and Joyce.*

HALEY: There was a wolf. Way up in the preserve. Out in the wind.

She had a den full of pups. She'd go out hunting by herself. Couldn't get anything big that way, mostly mice. Lemmings. She'd chew 'em up and then when she got back to the den she'd regurgitate them for the little ones. And they would nuzzle in her dark white

They hardly had any eyes.

And then one day she remembered something. She remembered something

And she started to go. She went. She was following that thing she could remember. She could smell it.

Through the snow. Down, following. Through the fields where there was snow. And she ate her own food without saving it.

And she kept moving down, down the map she didn't know about, that we know about

Finally over the border and into America.

And there still was snow. And she still kept moving, and eating, sometimes without eating. And without stopping.

What it was
that she remembered
As she came down
And the sun got warmer
And the snow disappeared
And the grass grew bright
And she came down
And the grass disappeared
And there was no more water, not so much
It was all white again
Where are they?

We have everything here.
Nothing gone
Nothing waiting
Whatever else there could have been is here and in plenty.

*Haley stands.*

So what is this
that I don't feel?
as she came down

And what
do I remember?

*Blackout. Only the Cube glows.*


*THE END*

Every Angel is Brutal

*Every Angel is Brutal* was first developed and produced as part of Summerworks at the Wild Project in May and June of 2016 by Clubbed Thumb, an Obie Award-winning company that commissions, develops, and produces funny, strange, and provocative new plays by living American playwrights. It was directed by Knud Adams and performed by Jihae Park, Susannah Perkins, Hubert Point-Du Jour, Jenny Seastone, Pete Simpson, and Amelia Workman. The set was by Marsha Ginsberg, costumes by Sydney Maresca, lighting by Bradley King, sound by Peter Mills-Weiss, and fight direction by Michael G. Chin; Production Stage Manager Sonja Thorson; Clubbed Thumb Producing Artistic Director Maria Striar.

## Characters

Clair, 19 and 20 years old, then 30 years old. American.

Jean, 20 years old, then 30 years old. American.

Lucy, 20 years old, also American. Later, Griffon Vulture, ancient/ageless.

Jochen, 38 years old, then 48 years old. German, but with just the barest trace of an accent. Tall and thin.

Lark, 19 and 20 years old. American. Energetic and pure of heart.

Klaus and Dennis, late 20s, German; Gerald, early 30s, American; Cuddeback, 50, Texan (all played by the same actor).

## Setting

Various locations around the USA and Berlin, Germany.

2002–2004 and, mostly, 2013–2014.

## Notes

A slash / in a line indicates that the following line starts at this point and overlaps with this one.

Line breaks might indicate either a rhythmic break or something like a cut between two takes of a film. They might also indicate that a song or a poem is being performed.

Translations of German words and phrases appear in brackets next to the line.

This play is an experiment in putting something like an action movie onstage. It should never stop being fun. Or almost never.

# Scene 1

*Winter 2002. An unassuming office somewhere near a college campus in America.*

*Clair, 19, enters. She looks around. She's well-dressed, for an interview, but flushed and a little disheveled, like someone who has just been doing something physically strenuous (which she has).*

*Clair sits down and hastily takes out a compact mirror. Small chuckle at her own appearance; she fixes it.*

*Puts the compact away. Breathes. Jochen enters and sits.*

JOCHEN: Hello Clair. I'm Jochen.

    You've done all the paperwork with Amanda, yes?

CLAIR: Yes.

JOCHEN: I hope the physical test wasn't too arduous.

CLAIR: No. What does that word mean again? No, I'm just kidding. No, it wasn't, it was fine.

JOCHEN: I'm recording this of course.

CLAIR: Of course.

JOCHEN: You assumed I would be recording it?

CLAIR: I did.

JOCHEN: Why?

CLAIR: Um. For your superiors.

JOCHEN: Who are my superiors?

CLAIR: The. Ultimately, the. CIA.

JOCHEN: The entire CIA?

CLAIR: No, of course not, just the superior part.

JOCHEN: I see.

CLAIR: Tenet! George J. Tenet.

JOCHEN: You think George Tenet will listen to the recording of this interview?

CLAIR: No, that's, I'm sure he won't.

JOCHEN: Would you like him to?

CLAIR: No.

JOCHEN: Why not?

CLAIR: Uh, I don't think it's going very well.

JOCHEN: Why not?

CLAIR: I'm saying all the wrong things.

JOCHEN: And why are you doing that?

CLAIR: I don't know.

JOCHEN: Do you often find that you say the wrong things?

CLAIR: Honestly, yes.

JOCHEN: That can be quite a liability.

CLAIR: Yeah no shit. I mean—

JOCHEN: On the other hand it can be an asset.

CLAIR: Really?

JOCHEN: If people think you're stupid, they'll let themselves be careless around you.

CLAIR: Guess that's good. If they're wrong.

JOCHEN: Are they wrong?

CLAIR: You mean am I stupid?

JOCHEN: Yes.

CLAIR: No. Yes, they're wrong.

JOCHEN: Am I wrong?

CLAIR: Uh. Well. Do you think I'm stupid?

JOCHEN: Why don't you let me ask the questions.

CLAIR: I'm sorry.

JOCHEN: Then I can figure out whether I think you're stupid. Or how stupid.

CLAIR: OK. Sounds great.

JOCHEN: You're very beautiful.

CLAIR: Thank you.

JOCHEN: Why do you want to do this work?

CLAIR: Everyone says Berlin is amazing...

JOCHEN: So everyone would like to do this work.

CLAIR: No, but. I can't imagine anyone—not feeling some kind of attraction...

JOCHEN: That's an interesting choice of words: does the prospect of this work excite you sexually?

CLAIR: Um. Sexually? I guess I'm not sure how I would distinguish. Between kinds of ex / citement.

JOCHEN: What do you think it entails?

*Beat.*

CLAIR: Being strong. Fast, clear. Knowing things that most people are not allowed to know. Playing some small part in the course of the actual history of the world.

*He looks at her.*

Doing things most people aren't allowed to do. And that they couldn't.

*Jochen shows Clair a photograph. She looks at it.*

JOCHEN: Would most people find that exciting?

*She keeps looking at the photo.*

I have to tell you that for every three agents we take on, there's one who doesn't make it.

*Clair looks up at him. She smiles.*

## Scene 2

*The following winter. "Set It Off" by Peaches plays. Nighttime at Klub de Republik, a cool bar in the Prenzlauer Berg neighborhood of Berlin. Clair is sitting with Klaus, about 28, German. They have to talk loudly over the music.*

CLAIR: We can speak in German if you want.

KLAUS: Wollen wir Deutsch sprechen? [Do we wanna speak German?]

CLAIR: Yeah.

KLAUS: Also ... sag was. [Then ... say something.]

CLAIR: Maybe later actually.

*Klaus laughs.*

KLAUS: Ok. It's good for me to practice English, I don't mind.

CLAIR: I'm the one who needs practice.

KLAUS: But you said you are taking courses at the Uni, and you have to speak German for these. I'm sure you are very ... that you speak very well.

CLAIR: Why?

KLAUS: I think you are an intelligent person.

CLAIR: Really? Why?

KLAUS: Your eyes.

CLAIR: Well then I fucked up.

KLAUS: What do you mean?

CLAIR: Uh, oh I just that's not the image that I'm interested in projecting.

KLAUS: I see. Why not?

CLAIR: It's not my angle.

KLAUS: Your Engel?

*(German for "angel.") He doesn't get it but moves on:*

But there are many different ways of being intelligent. Not every one is like a scientist.

How old are you actually?

CLAIR: Twenty.

*She smiles at him.*

Why don't you finish your beer.

KLAUS: OK. Why.

CLAIR: Maybe we could take a walk.

KLAUS: I would like this but I have to meet some people here.

CLAIR: I'm a person.

KLAUS: Yes. But these are a ... certain type of person. They're kind of dangerous. And we have to talk about serious things. You know what I mean?

CLAIR: How about just a walk around the Hof? [yard]

KLAUS: It's kind of cold.

CLAIR: Ohhh.

KLAUS: What.

CLAIR: I'm sorry. I understand. Don't feel bad.

KLAUS: Eh, no—

CLAIR: There's no reason to be embarrassed. I've known tons of guys with that problem. Especially here.

KLAUS: No.

*Klaus downs his beer.*

Let's go.

CLAIR: But if you—

KLAUS: No, let's go. We can go around the corner into the park very quick. You want to?

CLAIR: Yeah. Hold on.

*Klaus stands up.*

Just um, give me one second, I just remembered something.

KLAUS: You want to go?

CLAIR: I really do. But uh, I actually, I also have a problem. Ok it's called dyspareunia. Do you know what that is? It's just the name of a syndrome, you know—you know what a syndrome is?

KLAUS: Syn/drom...

CLAIR: Yeah it's basically a made-up disease where they don't actually know what they're talking about, just that a bunch of people have this overlapping set of problems, they don't know what causes it, it could be like completely different things, but they need a name for this problem, so. They call it a syndrome, and they give it a name, like dyspareunia, which—

*Klaus staggers.*

Why don't you sit down. Yeah, sit down here, it's ok.

*Klaus back in his seat. Meanwhile, Lucy and Jean, also 20 and American, appear at different corners of the room, watching.*

Dyspareunia is when sexual intercourse? Is like, super painful. Or just a little bit painful.

KLAUS: ...fühle mich nicht wohl ...[I don't feel so good...]

CLAIR: Why don't you just put your head down for a second.

*He does. Clair quickly makes eye contact with Lucy and Jean. Lucy gives a signal. Clair takes out a tiny electronic device and carefully clips it to Klaus's clothing somewhere. Jean takes out a receiver and holds it to her ear.*

Test.

*Jean gives the thumbs up. Clair ruffles Klaus's hair.*

Hey buddy. Hey new friend.

*Klaus doesn't respond. Whispering:*

I'm sorry you're gonna get lit up for wearing this. But you shouldn't be working for an arms dealer with a far-right agenda. Sweet boy like you.

*Clair pulls his head up and kisses him. He comes to and kisses her back.*

Tschüssi. [Bye-bye.]

*She exits. So do Lucy and Jean.*

KLAUS: There's something wrong with your vagina?

*He conks out. Lights down. Stereo Total's cover of Salt-N-Pepa's "Push It" plays loud.*

# Scene 3

*Later that night. The living room of the apartment in Mitte, Berlin that Clair, Jean, and Lucy are sharing during their semester abroad. The girls burst in, in high excitement. Jean might be a total square if she weren't so smart; ferociously competent, with maybe a hint of the soccer mom about her. Lucy is shifty and kind of androgynous, with a strange sweetness, like someone who might be able to talk to animals; she doesn't really know how to be a person yet. Clair is just Clair. At this moment, they're all feeling pretty fucking pleased with themselves.*

JEAN: But why do you say that? Of all the / things you could say—

CLAIR: Because it's confusing. Like they know they should pay attention 'cause it's something they're about to stick their dick in, but they have / no idea what any of it means—

JEAN: But what if you misjudged the dose even a little and he's not as far under as you think and he just gets turned off and walks / away?

CLAIR: I'm talking about my pussy, he's not gonna / "walk away."

JEAN: No, you know what it's like? It's like in movies when the bad guy has the hero tied up and—

LUCY: And the ties are treated with acid.

> *Jean and Clair stare at her.*

> So they start eating into his arms.

> *Beat.*

> Vaginal acid.

*Lucy laughs to herself. Clair and Jean exchange a glance, burst into laughter. Lucy laughs with them:*

> What? It's a rule of good conversation that, that, you can just, go to the next thing. You skip over the obvious thing and go to the next thing.

CLAIR: You do.

JEAN: Yeah, you sure do.

CLAIR: God, I feel so amped! Can't believe I have to go to class at ten. Maybe I'll
/ miss this one—
JEAN: No, you have to go.
LUCY: You should go.
CLAIR: Yeah fine.
JEAN: We'll make you some chamomile.
CLAIR: I'm gonna take a hot shower.

*As she exits, sings the line from NWA's "Dopeman":*

Wash out m'beaver!

*Jean checks the electric kettle for water and turns it on.*

LUCY: That was perfect.
JEAN: She's so good.
LUCY: So are you.
JEAN: So are you.
LUCY: Yeah I know, but. You're really, I mean . . . he really relies on you.
JEAN: Who, Jochen?
LUCY: *(Joke)* No, der Krampus.
JEAN: He relies on all of us, right?
LUCY: Yeah.
JEAN: He relies on you.
LUCY: Yeah.

*Pause. Jean gets the chamomile ready.*

JEAN: What?
LUCY: It's nice. Not to be alone.

*Jean looks at Lucy. Lucy is looking away. Jean goes to Lucy and gives her a kiss on the cheek.*

*At this point, there is a montage! Stereo Total's "Wir tanzen im 4-Eck" plays loud and we see brief moments and tableaux from the girls' dangerous, violent, glamorous life as highly trained spies who are posing as foreign exchange students in the world's coolest city. For instance, Lucy follows someone (unseen) down a dark street and out of sight, and then we hear an explosion. Jean uses a laptop to hack into the security system of a vault and then the three of them rush in. Lucy sits in class, taking notes in her notebook, but drifts off to sleep, and her book of Rilke poems falls on the floor. Jean and Clair both stand on the street, disguised as prostitutes; the target (invisible) approaches Clair; Jean follows them off. Lucy cleans a wound in Jean's leg while Jean bites down on a rag. You get the idea. Keep it moving, show a little, imply a lot, with lots of help from sound. The montage ends when the song does, and we're in...*

## Scene 4

*The apartment, a couple of months later: spring. Jean is lying on the couch, studying and eating from a large bag of Erdnußflips, which are like Cheetos only with peanut butter flavor instead of cheese. They're amazing and super gross. Clair enters.*

CLAIR: I swear to God, if one more alte Dame [old lady] scolds me, fucking scolds, as if that were a word that had any relevant application to the life of an adult.

JEAN: An adult you mean you?

CLAIR: What is the behaviorist bullshit in this country? What is this shocking fucking shocking credulity? Really if a little kid sees me cross the street against the light he will inevitably do the same? That's real dialectical. Take some responsibility.

JEAN: You're not an adult here. If you were German your parents would still be getting Kindergelt for you for seven more years.

CLAIR: What?

JEAN: Kindergelt.

CLAIR: What's that? Wait, they get—

JEAN: Yup.

CLAIR: Just for—

JEAN: Yup. The government pays you just for being young.

CLAIR: No way.

JEAN: Then they pay you for being old.

CLAIR: How do you know all this?

JEAN: It was in the packet.

CLAIR: Which one? Gimme an Erdnußflip.

*Jean passes Clair the Erdnußflips. Clair takes one, eats it. She eats more. With her mouth full:*

> God, they just melt in your mouth. Like Cheetos but with peanut butter. They're super disgusting. It's like I can feel them turning me bulimic.

JEAN: My cousin was bulimic.

CLAIR: I was for like a day. Is Lucy here?

JEAN: Haven't seen her.

CLAIR: I'm kinda worried about her.

*Jean stands up, takes the book and the Flips and proceeds towards her room.*

JEAN: I have to finish this.

CLAIR: When can we talk about Lucy?

JEAN: I don't know. Why, what?

CLAIR: You haven't noticed.

JEAN: That she's been in a bad mood?

CLAIR: We almost had to call it off last night. She wasn't gonna come.

JEAN: We could've gone without her.

CLAIR: We can't do anything / without all three of us.

JEAN: Without all three of us, I know.

CLAIR: So what the fuck? Has she said anything to you? You guys are always...

JEAN: Always what?

CLAIR: Has she?

JEAN: I think she's just . . . having some insecurities.

CLAIR: No idea what that means.

JEAN: No.

CLAIR: What'd she say?

JEAN: Look, I really have to finish this. Can we talk about it tomorrow?

CLAIR: Fine. I'll meet you after your class. We can get a beer.

JEAN: I love beer.

*Jean exits. Clair picks up her book again. She reads. She reaches for the Erdnuß-flips, which are no longer there. Lucy enters quietly from her bedroom. She is wearing a strange outfit; it should take us a minute to understand it's a kind of jogging outfit. Clair reads and Lucy watches her. Then Clair whips around.*

CLAIR: Oh hey! That's weird, I didn't hear you.

*Lucy says nothing.*

  What's up? How was class?

*Lucy says nothing.*

  What?

LUCY: What.

CLAIR: Nothing.

LUCY: What;

  what;

  what.

CLAIR: That's a . . . hip-hop thing . . . ?

LUCY: What's the worry that you have concerning me.

CLAIR: I'm sorry. I didn't mean to talk behind your back.

LUCY: You made a special date to talk behind my back.

CLAIR: No you just you seem really off this week.

LUCY: Off?

CLAIR: I just mean. I don't know. Maybe you should talk to Jochen.

LUCY: Jochen.

CLAIR: If you're feeling weird about something, or even just'r homesick, I'm sure it's not the first time someone's felt like / that in the program.

LUCY: You have no idea how I feel or how anyone feels. Look at you. You have no concern so don't pretend to be concerned.

CLAIR: I am concerned. Objectively. I'm involved.

*Jean enters.*

JEAN: Will you keep it down?

CLAIR: Lucy's home it turns out.

LUCY: Talk to me, not about me.

CLAIR: Oh get a sandwich board.

JEAN: Kinder! It's my turn to present in class and I'm filled with terror. What I need this day is quiet support, not a simulacrum of my home life.

CLAIR: Sorry Jean.

LUCY: You have my support.

JEAN: Thanks Lucy.

CLAIR: You'll do really great.

JEAN: But what if I've misunderstood everything?

*Jean goes back into her room.*

CLAIR: I just meant, that you might be . . . dealing with some personal issues that maybe cause you to act in a way that isn't completely cool. Not on purpose.

LUCY: Everything I do is on purpose.

CLAIR: Well yeah—

LUCY: And I am incredibly cool.

*Beat.*

CLAIR: You look like a freak. I've heard you crying. And those aren't pants.

LUCY: Let me tell you. In ten years, girls'll be going to school in tights only. And you will see this on the street and be amazed. And you'll talk to your thirty-year-old friends about it and you'll all be a little bit outraged and it won't even occur to you that this outrage means you've aged beyond any relevance to social progress. And late at night when you're alone, yes, alone, you'll suddenly remember that I predicted this and you'll think, I can't believe I thought she needed my insight!

CLAIR: Look—

LUCY: INSIGHT! FUCK!

*Lucy pulls out a long knife.*

CLAIR: What are you doing?

LUCY: Just. Give me your bank card.

CLAIR: Whh?

LUCY: Give me your bank card now, and don't make a sound. I'm rejecting this charade, I'm re—

CLAIR: JEAN!

*Jean enters with a gun.*

JEAN: Drop it Lucy.

LUCY: Listen. With all three cards we could empty the emergency account and get out of here—

CLAIR: Never!

LUCY: I'm not talking to you.

JEAN: Lucy, drop it.

CLAIR: Traitor.

JEAN: Shut up, Clair. Lucy. It's gonna be ok.

*Jean shoots Lucy in the arm. Lucy howls and drops the knife. Clair retrieves it.*

CLAIR: I'll call Jochen.

LUCY: You
     are gonna feel so
     bad

## Scene 5

*A basement office. Jochen and Lucy. Her arm is bandaged; she is cuffed and subdued; thirsty. Jochen clicks something and we hear a recorded conversation between Lucy and JEAN:*

JEAN: You sound kind of crazy. I think, I think you're jumping to conclusions.

LUCY: I saw him.

JEAN: But what did you really see?

LUCY: I saw him slit that woman's throat!

*Jochen touches his own throat.*

JEAN: She must've been an enemy agent.

LUCY: Oh come on! She was a, a junkie hooker, she could hardly / put two words together—

JEAN: Why don't you ask him about it? He probably knows you saw him.

LUCY: Oh God. / No, I don't—

JEAN: Just ask him. I'm sure there's an explanation. And he might not be able to tell you, but he'll, he can let you know that it's ok. It's no worse than, than plenty of other stuff we've been doing. Stuff you've been doing. The two oh four last week? That little old guy must've been eighty, and you sliced him like a hard-boiled egg and dumped him face-down in the Panke.

This is the dirty work. Right?

LUCY: Would you come with me?

JEAN: Where?

LUCY: Estonia.

JEAN: That's crazy.

LUCY: Stop saying that! I'm right or I'm wrong, but I'm not crazy.

JEAN: Look. Just take a breath. And acknowledge that what we're doing is stressful and can affect us in ways that—

LUCY: Jean, please—

JEAN: Why don't you give yourself a week. Ok? Just as an experiment.

LUCY: I don't know, I've been thinking about this a lot and there are other things too, things that don't make sense. Like—

JEAN: Stop. Can you hear yourself? This is exactly what they talked about at orientation. The doubts. It's like you're repeating them word for word.

LUCY: I . . . am I?

JEAN: Give yourself a little time to sit with it before you do anything. All right?

*Beat.*

LUCY: Ok.

*Beat.*

But if I...

JEAN: What?

LUCY: If I can't sit with it, if I figure out I'm right and I can't...
and I have to...

*Beat.*

I care about you very much.

Can you tell that?

JEAN: Sure. I care about you too.

*The recording ends.*

JOCHEN: Have you ever been to Estonia?

I don't recommend it.

Lucy, I thought things were going so well. I thought maybe this is the year
when I don't lose anyone. I would have been so proud.

*Lucy snorts.*

But you saw something you didn't like and so you try to undermine morale.
You know that's treason.

What are we going to do with you?

*Lucy sniffs.*

Guess.

*No answer.*

Guess.

LUCY: I already know.

JOCHEN: I don't think so.

*Pause. Jochen looks off to the side. Light out.*

*More music. Ten years are passing.*

*Sound: we hear bits of news items in the mix with the music, something about the* depression, something about drugs, something about sex trafficking (maybe a clip from *"Taken"*). We hear a clip from the Food Channel show *"Cupcake Attack."* We might also hear little clips from other movies and TV shows. Something about Merkel finding out that the U.S. spies on Germany and being outraged, i.e., it's 2013.

*Meanwhile: We see Jean in her small apartment in non-coastal Florida. She wears practical, unfashionable clothes and an apron. She sits on the couch. Maybe she holds a Tom Clancy novel in her lap. She remembers something, looks up, and smiles to herself. Her smile fades.*

*We see Clair and her husband Gerald, 32, settling into their apartment in a large Midwestern city. Clair opens a Tom Clancy novel and removes a five-ounce bag of cocaine from its hollowed-out inside. She begins weighing out the coke in grams.*

## Scene 6

*Just outside the airport of the large Midwestern city. Late at night. Autumn. Gerald, an airport employee, is waiting for the shuttle.*

*Jean, who is now 30 but looks older, has come out of the airport with a rolling suitcase. Gerald glances towards her, smiles politely, and goes back to waiting for the shuttle. Jean comes up—just a little bit closer to Gerald than is strictly customary—and waits for the shuttle beside him. Throughout the scene, she remains cheerful, without the slightest sense of awkwardness.*

*Gerald tells himself silently that there's no way she's anything to worry about.*

JEAN: I can still get the bus here, right?
GERALD: Which bus is that.
JEAN: The bus to the train?
GERALD: The shuttle? Yup, that stops right here, that's what I'm waiting for.
JEAN : Great.

*Gerald begins to relax. Then something occurs to him.*

GERALD: You just coming out now?

JEAN: Excuse me?

GERALD: Airport's been closed the last hour. Not s'posed to be any customers left.

JEAN: Oh I know. I got really lost in there. I kept going around in circles.

GERALD: You can always ask someone to point you / towards the exit.

JEAN: And then I had a stomach emergency, so I had to take a detour to the bathroom, and hang out there for a while. I'm sorry, I interrupted you.

GERALD: That's ok.

    You feeling better?

JEAN: Much. It was a little scary though, because they kept making the announcements and I was afraid I'd get trapped in there overnight, but. You can't really rush that stuff.

GERALD: You wouldn't of gotten locked in. Someone woulda found you. Only thing is there mighta been a security concern.

JEAN: Oh, you mean it would've been suspicious?

GERALD: Well, we / have to—

JEAN: And there I went and flushed all the evidence in my defense.

GERALD: Huh

JEAN: Are you airport security? You said "we."

GERALD: I work with everyone. Communications.

JEAN: A-ha! Good gig. Lots of growth opportunities.

*This response unnerves Gerald, who was just beginning to feel comfortable.*

GERALD: Ma'am, would you mind showing me some ID?

JEAN: I'm Jean.

GERALD: I'd just feel better if I took your information. In case anything / comes up later—

JEAN: Oh oh, I getcha, sure, no problem,—

*She squints at his ID badge.*

    Gerald.

*She takes her wallet out of her purse and hands him her driver's license.*

This way if they find a cherry bomb in there, right?

*He looks at her. She looks back at him.*

GERALD: Right.

*He looks at her driver's license.*

Florida.

JEAN: Cross City!

Ever been?

*He shakes his head no and hands it back to her.*

It's a complicated place.

*They wait for the shuttle.*

JEAN: You ok Gerald?

GERALD: It's just been a long day. Shuttle should be—ope, there it is now.

*We hear the shuttle approaching.*

JEAN: You know what? I'm still not feeling too great, I think I'm gonna take a cab.

GERALD: Cabs've mostly gone by now.

JEAN: Isn't that one over there? Yeah, that looks like a cab. But I can't tell if he's still on duty.

GERALD: You know, ma'am, I really gotta—

JEAN: You think you could just take a look for me? I'll stand here and make sure Ambrose doesn't leave without you.

*Gerald reluctantly heads off towards the cab stand.*

Thank you!

*As soon as Gerald is gone, Jean tosses something towards the shuttle. Gerald reappears.*

GERALD: How do you know Ambrose?

JEAN: I'm an idiot!

*Jean runs at Gerald and sacks him. The shuttle explodes.*

*Beat.*

*Jean raises her head. She surveys the damage. She beams.*

*She jumps up, almost dancing with glee. She tugs on Gerald.*

Ok. You're ok. Right? Ok. Let's go.

*With her help, Gerald staggers to his feet.*

Did I hurt you? Come on.

*Gerald stands motionless, staring at the exploded shuttle.*

GERALD: Is that

JEAN: No, not at all. Come on, mister.

GERALD: Who

JEAN: We're friends of your wife's. Don't look at that. Listen, Ambrose was a slimeball. He was not your buddy. I'm taking you home.

*Gerald, dazed, lets her lead him off. Sirens sound.*

## Scene 7

*The apartment where Clair and Gerald live. Clair is standing by the window, looking out. Also ten years older, naturally, but looks pretty much the same. She stares out the window, trying to see into the dark. At last she makes a phone call. Voicemail. Clair looks out the window as she leaves the message. Impromptu code.*

CLAIR: Hey Ger, I hope you get this, you remember how I'd seen that um, weird "dog" outside a few days ago, kinda watching the building? Like standing at the corner? Well, don't freak out, but it was out there again this afternoon, I . . . know you don't like dogs so I wanted to warn you. In case you were carrying any . . . "meat," or anything?

*She hangs up. Looks out. Maybe she only thinks this:*

Who are you?

*She crosses to a desk, opens the top drawer, takes out a gun. Checks it. Phone rings. She puts the gun away, answers the phone.*

Hey, d'you listen to my—

Ger?

*Light up on Jean and Gerald in a car which Jean is driving, and which is swerving slightly because Jean has just reached over to grab Gerald's phone.*

JEAN: Don't complicate things.

*He reaches across her for the phone; she holds it out the window, threatening to drop it.*

GERALD: Fuck

JEAN: Sit down, please.

*Gerald sits down, puts his head in his hands. Jean watches the road. They ride.*

What would you like to know?

GERALD: Who are you?

JEAN: You saw my driver's license.

GERALD: What do you want?

JEAN: I just need to talk to Clair.

GERALD: If you try to hurt her—

JEAN: Ha! No. She'll be glad to see me. I promise.

GERALD: Why'd you do that?

*He starts to freak out again.*

JEAN: Shh. You guys really have to be more careful. Frankly I'm a little scandalized. If I were married and my husband went around bragging about our dirty little sideline to every bus driver who bought him a beer, ours would not be a happy marriage. No offense.

GERALD: What?

JEAN: The two of you could not be making it easier. A couple months of totally standard remote surveillance and I know more about your business than you do. Ambrose was wearing a wire tonight. Guess why.

GERALD: Uh

JEAN: Your friend was big into kiddie porn. Yup, and those guys are beyond desperate. You got on the shuttle, he was gonna draw you out, get you on tape naming names, and then break it out the first time he needed leverage. And then you and Clair are both "in the slammer" or "up the river" or whatever you hardened criminal types are calling it these days.

GERALD: L—leverage?

JEAN: Bet you didn't think of that when you offered to "cut him in." Really screwed up our timing, too. We were gonna take it slow. After all, I haven't spoken to Clair in ten years.

GERALD: Ten years?

You're CIA.

JEAN: Did Clair tell you she was CIA?

GERALD: Not exactly.

JEAN: That's my girl. I'm so excited to see her. I kept saying first things first, we've gotta find Clair.

GERALD: She never mentioned you.

JEAN: Well we were very close.

I bet I know her better than you do.

GERALD: I've been inside her.

JEAN: That's so gross, Gerald.


# Scene 8

*Light change: now they are in the apartment with Clair. Jean and Clair stare at each other. Gerald watches them both. Pause.*

CLAIR: You look like shit.
JEAN: Well, I'm old.

CLAIR: That's no excuse.

JEAN: You don't look like shit. You look great.

CLAIR: I spend a lot of money on products.

*Beat.*

    Aw, girl!

*Clair and Jean hug.*

GERALD: She blew up Ambrose!

CLAIR: Who?

GERALD: The shuttle.

CLAIR: What?

GERALD: Ambrose's shuttle, just...

CLAIR: Baby, are you ok?

GERALD: I'm fine, I'm fine—

CLAIR: *(To Jean)* You blew something up? At the airport?

JEAN: Not inside.

CLAIR: What's going on?

GERALD: She's CIA.

*Jean and Clair exchange a glance.*

CLAIR: I've told him a little bit about my government work.

GERALD: You said it was over.

CLAIR: It was.

JEAN: Well, look.

CLAIR: So they ... kept you active?

*Beat.*

JEAN: No.

CLAIR: Oh. Ok.

GERALD: Wait.

JEAN: I've actually been working in food service.

GERALD: So—

CLAIR: *(To Jean)* Shut up.

JEAN: What?

CLAIR: "Food service." I saw.

*Jean blushes.*

JEAN: What...

CLAIR: *(Confessing)* I saw ya on the television.

JEAN: Cupcake Attack? You watch that show?

CLAIR: Your shit looked delicious! What was it, cardamom—

JEAN: Cardamom with cream cheese frosting.

CLAIR: I was so happy for you.

JEAN: That's nice, Clair.

CLAIR: I couldn't believe you lost.

*Beat.*

JEAN: I came in second.

CLAIR: You think that was smart, though? To go on TV like that?

JEAN: Well, I look different now. As you pointed out.

GERALD: EXCUSE ME

*They look at him.*

      WHAT IS HAPPENING

CLAIR: You know what, um

*Beat.*

GERALD: What.

CLAIR: Maybe you should lie down—

GERALD: Lie down? Fuck you, Clair. And fuck this . . . terrorist Rachael Ray. I can't—I'm—I better leave.

JEAN: Rachael Ray?

GERALD: [I'll] be at the bar.

*Gerald leaves. Clair calls after him:*

CLAIR: Wait. Did you get my message? About the dog?

*Gerald returns, unzipping his jacket. He removes a large parcel and tosses it to Clair, then exits. She puts it away in the drawer.*

JEAN: Copyediting, right? I saw your website.

CLAIR: He does my website. Sorry he's—

JEAN: That's ok. Rachael Ray's pretty amazing. I'd rather be Giada, but.

CLAIR: *(Distracted)* I'm Giada.

He's gonna get drunk...

JEAN: It's ok. Someone's on him.

CLAIR: Arright, bitch, give it up.

JEAN: Well. So. It's funny that you mention Cupcake Attack. Actually you're not the only one who saw it.

CLAIR: Jochen?

JEAN: *(Laughing)* No! Can you imagine him watching—? I mean who knows, but. No. Someone else.

*Beat.*

CLAIR: Wait. They let her out?

JEAN: She escaped.

CLAIR: Where is she now?

*Beat. Clair realizes something, gasps, goes back to the window, peers out.*

Shit. That was Lucy.

JEAN: Yes and no.

*A pair of hands reach out from under the couch. Or are they claws? SOMETHING hoists itself up into view just as the lights go out.*

*Julia Jarcho*

## Scene 9

*Gerald and Lark, 19, at the neighborhood bar. They have just met. Gerald is doing his best to get a little drunk. At no time does Lark manifest even a trace of irony.*

GERALD: I guess it should be all right with me but, I don't know, yeah, should it be? I don't know.

LARK: I don't know.

GERALD: I mean how old are you?

LARK: Not that old.

GERALD: No, so. But what do you think? Really?

LARK: Gosh.

GERALD: It's not that I don't want her to be. Three-dimensional.

LARK: No of course not.

GERALD: God, sorry, I been rambling. I should leave you alone. Thank you for humoring me.

LARK: That's all right.

GERALD: You don't, uh, forgive me, you don't seem like you're native to these parts. That's not a like a pickup line, I just, ah, fuckit.

LARK: I live in the hills.

*Beat.*

GERALD: What?

LARK: The hill country.

GERALD: Oh, like Texas?

LARK: Yes, like that.

GERALD: Country girl. Woman.

LARK: Simple people.

GERALD: That's cool. I mean it's a joke, that's a joke, right? There's no simple people actually.

LARK: We try to be.

GERALD: Huh. Me too. Me too all the time. That's why she likes me. I know that's why.

LARK: Clair?

GERALD: God, I'm sorry, I'm talking your ear off. Maybe I should just leave. Should I leave? Just go back there and deal with her weird old terrorist friend?

*Lark has surreptitiously checked her watch.*

LARK: I'm gonna have another drink.

*Gerald smiles at her gratefully.*


## Scene 10

*Clair's apartment. Clair and Jean have now been joined by Griffon Vulture, who was once Lucy. Griffon looks as if Lucy had been torn to pieces and had sewn herself back together again using the darkest arts of taxidermy, i.e., she has a certain glamor.*

*Pause.*

JEAN: Let's all sit down.

*They don't.*

CLAIR: Good to see you, Lucy.

*Beat.*

JEAN: She doesn't go by that name anymore. It's—

*Griffon Vulture turns her head sharply to face Jean.*

Griffon Vulture.

CLAIR: That's cool. It's like a code name.

GRIFFON: Do not try and decode it.

*Beat.*

CLAIR: So . . .

JEAN: Griffon got in touch with me. After she saw the show.

CLAIR: And you just . . . came to town, to say hi?

JEAN: Ambrose was a fifty-eight. For you.

CLAIR: No kidding. And how'd you figure that out? And how'd you find me?

*Griffon Vulture makes a sound that is probably a laugh.*

Unh-huh.

*As Clair talks, she starts edging toward the drawer that holds the gun.*

You guys mind if I smoke? I don't do it a lot, just for . . . special occasions. This is a little overwhelming—

GRIFFON: Look in my eyes.

CLAIR: Why.

JEAN: Griffon—

GRIFFON: Look in my aaaheeesclaaaair

*This last word rises continuously and musically in pitch until it ends as a mighty shriek, against which Clair is helpless. She looks into Griffon's eyes.*

This is not magic
Rather is it of science an unexpected application
Who if you cried would hear you
Out the angel orders? (Don't answer.)
Take I you suddenly against my breast you DISSIPATE,
Clair, last of that hideous name.
All others have shattered against my resolve
My effluvium stronger than steel
Stronger than foxes of stone.

*Clair staggers. She falls onto the couch. As if in a trance:*

CLAIR: It means light...

JEAN: It's not that I'm not impressed, but.

*Griffon looks down at Clair.*

I'm the one who shot you.

GRIFFON: You did not believe me. She would not even have understood me. That is much worse.

*Pause.*

Jean...
How was
your flight?

## Scene 11

*Gerald and Lark at the bar.*

GERALD: Why're you so nice? I'm not like a real fascinating guy.

LARK: I understand about feelings, that's all.

GERALD: Yeah, I can tell.

LARK: And I also love someone who is ...complicated.

GERALD: Why can't they all be simple like us?

LARK: *(Answering the question)* God.

GERALD: We met at a bar fight. I don't know. I was in the fight. Someone ...said something about ...Albanians? I got a tooth knocked loose. Bruised up. Really just gross. She followed me out. I'd noticed her before. She followed me out, I could not of been more surprised. Blood. On my shirt. Turns out that's what she, she's a, like a...

*Shakes his head.*

LARK: Angel?

GERALD: Ha ha, yeah. She is beautiful. Well, you know what that's like, you're beautiful.

*Raises his glass.*

To the ladies.

*Lark clinks his glass with hers.*

LARK: To the ladies.

*Gerald drinks. Lark watches him.*


## Scene 12


*Clair's apartment. Clair sits bolt upright and gasps.*

JEAN: Feeling better?

CLAIR: *(To Griffon)* What the fuck did you do to me, you freak?

*Jean holds Clair's parcel disparagingly:*

JEAN: Really?

CLAIR: Jesus, it's better than fucking cupcakes.

JEAN: Do you know how many American women dream of opening a cupcake bakery? Last year there was a survey done, and it turns out pretty much everyone—

GRIFFON: It has been painful for both you these years. Waiting.

JEAN & CLAIR: I haven't been / waiting—

GRIFFON: Waiting for the call, the tap on the shoulder from a stranger, the folded note on the sill, even the hypodermic prick of a passing assassin would have been better than the empty years, your hair growing thin, your waist growing thick. [CLAIR: Ha!] What was Jean's appearance on Cupcake Attack but a desperate attempt to attract their attention once more.

JEAN: I needed PR for the shop.

GRIFFON: And have you never wondered why, after your exemplary service, your country has left you to fend for yourself?

CLAIR: Wasn't in it for the pension plan.

GRIFFON: No, not. And yet you thought, as you embarked on your sordid little venture, that someone would drive up in a black automobile. Roll down the window and whisper: Clair, this is beneath you! We have more important things lined up!

CLAIR: No, Lucy, I didn't. I'm actually happy now. I have a home and someone who loves me. Who I love. I'm fine.

JEAN: "Someone who loves me who I love, I'm fine"??

CLAIR: You know what? It wasn't gonna happen! We were never gonna get another call. Because of *(to Griffon)* you. Your little meltdown, that's why they freezed us out.

JEAN: *(Under her breath)* Froze.

GRIFFON: Who freezed you out?

CLAIR: The agency. Jochen. My fucking country, yes, ok?

GRIFFON: There is no my country.

CLAIR: Right, 'cause you're a citizen of the world now. Halloween World.

JEAN: Look: he wasn't—we weren't—

*Glances at Griffon.*

there was no State connection.

CLAIR: What—

JEAN: We weren't working for the government. Clair, I . . . checked it out. Really thoroughly. It's true.

*Pause.*

CLAIR: Wait. Wait. Stop. So . . .

JEAN: We were never spies. Just thugs.

GRIFFON: Criminals working for a criminal.

CLAIR: No. The whole apparatus . . . the training . . . the recruitment—

JEAN: The shabby little rented offices weren't a front. They were shabby little rented offices.

CLAIR: The training—the resources—the technology—

GRIFFON: All obtainable on the free market.

CLAIR: Sure, but that's what they told us they'd say. If anything went wrong they'd tank the program and deny knowledge. There were whole sectors of the structure that couldn't even know / about the—

*Griffon Vulture reveals a horrible scar.*

*The others stare.*

*Pause.*

But we were so good.

## Scene 13

*Flashback: Autumn 2004. Office of a defunct warehouse somewhere in the suburbs of Berlin. Jochen and Cuddeback, an American businessman. Cuddeback is peering out through a glass window at the warehouse floor.*

CUDDEBACK: I don't see her.

JOCHEN: Along the back wall. The left hand corner.

CUDDEBACK: Oh I took that for a pile of refuse.

*He looks.*

She know I'm here?

JOCHEN: I don't always know what she knows. Difficult passageways.

*Cuddeback is about to object.*

In her mind.

CUDDEBACK: *(Relieved)* You not much of a salesman. You're workin for me, I'd fire you.

JOCHEN: I think the merchandise will speak for itself.

CUDDEBACK: It's been five months, you said. She malnourished?

JOCHEN: And without open wounds. You'll find a lot of scarring.

CUDDEBACK: That's fine.

JOCHEN: You'll want to be careful about reintroducing rich foods. Or anyway mindful.

CUDDEBACK: Hnh. We keep it simple on the ranch. Simple pastoral pleasures. Ever been to the hill country?

JOCHEN: Well you may want to administer antibiotics. Depending on your time-line.

CUDDEBACK: What'd she do to you anyway?

JOCHEN: As I told you I don't consider it necessary to discuss that.

*Jochen signals. Lucy enters.*

CUDDEBACK: Huh.

JOCHEN: They're usually much more . . . conventionally good-looking. You can think of this as a one-time opportunity.

*Cuddeback walks around Lucy, looking at her.*

CUDDEBACK: Look at those bones. Come over here, honey.

JOCHEN: She'll try to kill you.

CUDDEBACK: No shit!

LUCY: You speak about someone who is standing in the room with us.

CUDDEBACK: I didn't mean to be rude.

LUCY: Standing in the room with us but not where you think.

JOCHEN: She's naturally somewhat dissociated.

CUDDEBACK: Reminds me of a little dead bird.

(*To Lucy*) Hey bird.

*He peers at one of her wounds.*

What happened there?

LUCY: You speak about a body that doesn't exist.

CUDDEBACK: Yeah. This is it. This is good. I had a dog once—can she understand us?

JOCHEN: Can you understand us, Lucy?

LUCY: You speak about someone

*Beat.*

CUDDEBACK: So this dog I had
hunting dog
watch dog

had him trained him up in a pit by himself from a pup
every time I saw him he'd go right for my throat
went for my throat every time, whole life.
And finally when we had to put him down, he was lookin up at me, not at
my eyes, was lookin up at my throat, full of tenderness,
wanting to tear it out
good animal
I still have the pit where I raised him
it's been empty

*Silence while Cuddeback and Lucy look at each other and Jochen observes them both.*

Yeah I'll take her.

LUCY: He knows it's a mistake.

CUDDEBACK: You're gonna have to learn to pipe down, baby bird. Baby bird dog baby dog you'll learn.

JOCHEN: Your men can come for her this evening before you fly.
All the documentation is in place. She's an exchange student from Arizona State.

CUDDEBACK: No shit. My niece went there. Maybe they were in the same sorority. What'd you say her name was?

JOCHEN: Lucy.

CUDDEBACK: "Lucy."
Huh.

*Blackout.*

# Scene 14

*Clair's apartment.*

JEAN: Lucy.

GRIFFON: Lucy was a foreign exchange student from Arizona State. LUCY was very EXCITED to explore the world-famous Berlin NIGHTLIFE and to decorate her BEDROOM with posters of the DOOMED POLAR BEAR CUB KNUT

JEAN: I think Knut was later...

CLAIR: Whatever, Jesus!

GRIFFON: They kept me unconscious for the entire flight. I woke up in the back seat of a sports utility vehicle riding over miles of country to the ranch. There were only three of them; they should have tied me tighter. Jochen had warned them after all.

JEAN: The training was good for something.

GRIFFON: The training was good. I roamed the hill country for a week, covered in their blood. I fed off a den of coyote pups. I thought I would change into an animal. I thought that I had always been an animal. Only my body would have killed me, this body that followed me still with its craven sub-animal terror of pain. And so after eight days and nights, I applied at the Compound of the Star Valley Moon Pigeon Cousins of Christ. At first they regarded me with some unease. But as was consistent with their beliefs they agreed to house me and feed me; and later to accept my counsel when I offered it unsought; and then to seek it; and ultimately, after some years, to bestow on me the title of Elder and my own daughter-wife.

*Lark appears in flashback.*

And in honor of that sacred event, and to show the extent of their trust: a television.

*As Griffon Vulture talks, the apartment becomes her cabin at the Compound. The sound of crickets and a slightly static-y TV fade up under her speech.*

After a morning of fasting and incantation, an afternoon spent in collo-quy with the troubled, and an evening of communal repair, young bride at my side I would settle in to enjoy an hour of something like pleasure. The themes of the challenges amused me: "ice skating"; "Hollywood"; "racial difference." How might the contestants express such various longings in something so abject as a cup-sized cake? And then one day:

*In flashback, Jean speaks as if from the TV:*

JEAN: I'm disappointed. To come so far and not win is a definitely a bummer. It would've been really good for us to get to go serve cupcakes to Liam Nee-son and that girl who plays his daughter. And the money would've helped a lot of course. We'll probably have to close the shop soon, since everyone's already getting sick of cupcakes.

*As this speech goes on, Griffon Vulture leans closer and closer to the television, peering. At first she's overcome with joy to see her old friend . . .*

But someone has to be eliminated.

*A brutal awakening begins to take hold. Memories flood over the Griffon. She begins to rise.*

Anyway, I had a great time, I really challenged myself and took risks and thanks for the opportunity.

LARK: Mother Vulture? Everything all right?

*In the welter of noises Griffon hears, one sentence from the Cupcake Attack clip we just heard repeats itself, quietly at first, then more insistently: "But someone has to be eliminated."*

GRIFFON: Every three...

He said: for every three...

*Jochen appears.*

JOCHEN: I have to tell you that for every three agents we take on, there's one who doesn't make it.

*Flashback over; back in Clair's apartment.*

CLAIR: Every three.

JEAN: Every year.

GRIFFON: It was not only you I had failed to protect. But the three who came after. And the three after that. Of which there must always be one.

CLAIR: Tortured?

JEAN: Sold. To fund the next three.

GRIFFON: And so on forever.

*Clair is stunned. Back to Lark and Gerald at the bar, where Lark is checking the time. Gerald more drunk.*

GERALD: I told her you don't have to tell me. I like for there to be something hidden inside you like a, you know. Keeps it . . . it keeps it . . .

LARK: People like us look for different kinds of communities.

GERALD: I don't know what that means.

LARK: All I'm saying is, we've suffered and, we want things. We cannot be faulted but we can be preserved, from, the most marauding of our desires, through discipline and . . .

GERALD: Don't say prayer.

LARK: Why not? My vulture showed me. Here, let me walk you home.

GERALD: Your what?

LARK: My mother. My true heart. Come on.

*They exit. Back in the apartment, Clair is distraught.*

CLAIR: So do we . . . go to Washington? Talk to the feds? The real ones?

GRIFFON: Are you keen to attract the eye of the law?

CLAIR: Well what're we gonna do, go back there and stop him?

*She didn't really mean it, but . . .*

JEAN: You were the best at at eighty-four, seventeen, one oh six . . .

CLAIR: Wait—seriously?

GRIFFON: "We can't do anything without all three . . ."

CLAIR: But—it's been ten years.

It was hormones that made us wanna do that stuff before. Right?

I don't remember any of it, really, I'm so out of shape…
And besides, how're we supposed to get to him?

*Lark bursts in with Gerald.*

LARK: Mother vulture!

JEAN: That's how.

GRIFFON: Together we will make her irresistible to him.

LARK: I want to be something wonderful and terrible. Please help me.

*Gerald takes in the scene in front of him, and exits.*

*Blackout.*


## Scene 15

*Sound of someone breathing hard, working out. Lights rise slowly on Lark and Griffon Vulture. Griffon is practicing with Lark, training her in a martial and mental art which is neither Eastern nor Western. Then music comes up full blast and the scene becomes—guess what? Another montage! Yes, a training montage, and it is fucking cool, and not a parody. Some things that happen: A shooting drill where Clair yells out in code what to fire at and Lark fires:*

CLAIR: Spielplatz! [Playground]

> *Lark fires.*

> > S-Bahn! [Street-level train]

> *Lark fires.*

> > Lark!

LARK: What?

CLAIR: No!

LARK: No—sorry!

CLAIR: Spargelzeit! [Asparagus season]

*Lark fires.*

    Zoo escape!

*Lark fires.*

    Lark!

LARK: No!

CLAIR: What's your name?

LARK: Sophie

*Lark fires.*

    Berkowitz.

*Lark fires.*

*Another part of the montage: Lark, kneeling on the floor, assembles a bomb while Jean, kneeling next to her, times her with a stopwatch. Once Lark finishes, Jean resets the stopwatch and nods to her. Lark starts taking apart the bomb. She is about to unclip a particular wire when Jean shoves her violently to prevent her, and shows her the right way to proceed. Lark continues disassembling the bomb;*

*Another part: Clair, Jean, and Lark all practice running. Lark eventually races off ahead of Clair and Jean;*

*And: Lark disassembling a bomb again, this time blindfolded. Clair, Jean, and Griffon stand around her. Lark makes a mistake; Clair goes to stop her; Griffon holds Clair back. Lark fixes the mistake;*

*And more. The montage ends with Lark doing sit-ups alone in Clair's apartment.*

## Scene 16

*Nighttime. Lark doing sit-ups alone in the apartment. Gerald enters, coming home from work. He carries a black plastic bag from a convenience store. Takes out a box of peanut butter Cap'n Crunch and a carton of milk. He gets a bowl and a spoon. He opens the Cap'n Crunch, pours some into the bowl, opens the milk, pours some into the bowl, stares at it, sits down with bowl and spoon, begins to eat. Meanwhile Lark has stopped and is resting on her back. Silence. Crunch, crunch.*

GERALD: Don't let me disturb you.

*Lark sits up.*

LARK: Sorry, I'll get out of your way.

GERALD: Don't mind me of all people.

*Lark does a quick stretch as she talks. She is guileless, and energetic even though she has been working very hard.*

LARK: They're all up in number 5D. I just came down here for the quiet. But I'll go back. How was your day?

GERALD: Dull.

LARK: No cocaine today?

GERALD: Excuse me?

*Beat.*

No cocaine, no.

LARK: In case it were to cause a complication in the plan.

GERALD: I guess everyone has his own perspective on what complicates and what gets complicated.

LARK: I'll go up and tell Clair you're here, should I?

GERALD: I texted her.

LARK: What is that?

GERALD: Horrible cereal. You never had this kind before?

LARK: "Peanut butter cappin crunch." It's horrible?

GERALD: It's delicious, in a horrible way. But it's not for you, you're training.

LARK: I want to try it. I'm supposed to practice "identifying what I want in a given situation." It's part of the training.

GERALD: That's interesting.

LARK: At the Compound we don't really think that way.

*Impulsively, she sticks her hand into the cereal box and pulls out some Crunch. She looks down at it in her hand.*

Maybe I don't want it.

*She drops the cereal back into the box. Pause.*

I don't mind.

GERALD: What?

LARK: The cocaine.

*Beat.*

GERALD: Why, you want some?

LARK: Ha ha.

GERALD: What do you mean you don't mind.

LARK: Nothing.

GERALD: What do you mean?

LARK: Just none of us upstairs . . . has any objections or . . . looks down on—

GERALD: Who the fuck are any of you to have / "objections"?

LARK: Nobody! Nobody!

GERALD: This is the kind of shit that mortals do. I'm sorry to disappoint you.

LARK: But I'm saying the opposite, I'm saying it doesn't disappoint me. But that sounds wrong too! I think it's good. People need to feel something, you help them.

GERALD: I just get it through security.

LARK: I'm being stupid. Forgive me. My interview on campus is tomorrow, you know. And after that it won't be safe to come back here. And then if everything goes well . . . have you ever been to Berlin?

GERALD: No.

LARK: Well. I might not see you again. Good night!

*She exits. Gerald calls after her.*

GERALD: Lark!

*Lark comes back. He's not sure what to say.*

How old are you?

LARK: Why?

GERALD: I just think that . . . maybe it's not fair. For you to have to do something so dangerous.

LARK: I'm twenty like they were. Clair was.

GERALD: You're not like Clair.

LARK: That hurts my feelings a little.

GERALD: Clair's just. . .

She doesn't like to be bored. You're not bored.

LARK: I'm never bored. I'm in love.

GERALD: Right.

LARK: Vulture saved me. Every day she saves me.

GERALD: You don't seem to need it.

LARK: You don't know.

GERALD: I don't, but. . .

LARK: No. You just don't.

*Beat. Gerald wants to ask Lark what she had to be saved from, but he can't quite muster the courage.*

Can I have some?

*It takes Gerald a moment to see what she means. Then he takes out a gram of coke from the drawer with the gun. He gives her some. She snorts it. He watches her.*

You too?

*Gerald takes some. They sit there, not looking at each other.*

GERALD: Well?

LARK: It's nice.

GERALD: Good.

LARK: It is, isn't it?

GERALD: Yeah, it's nice.

*Beat.*

LARK: Because of the violence that happened to Griffon Vulture I'm not allowed to with her. You know?

*Beat.*

> We love each other and I'm her wife and I'm not allowed to. But what I have to do tomorrow, and after, that will be hard. That will be hard hard, hard.
>
> And I think it's the closest thing.
>
> You know?

*Gerald looks at her.*

GERALD: So you're her wife ... and her daughter.

LARK: That's what we call it.

GERALD: Oh God.

LARK: Hard.

*They kiss. They make out.*

*Then Clair enters, followed by Jean and Griffon. Gerald jumps up, horrified. Lark smiles brightly.*

CLAIR: *(To Lark)* Very nice.

GERALD: *(To Clair)* Baby, it's my fault.

JEAN: Very nice!

GERALD: Clair, let's talk. Could you guys just give us a minute alone?

CLAIR: That's ok baby. Really.

*Lark unclips the device Clair used in Scene 2, which Lark has managed to attach to Gerald's clothes somewhere, and hands it to Jean, who puts it away, helps herself to some Cap'n Crunch, and exits. Griffon holds out a hand to Lark. Lark, beaming, holds her hand out to Griffon's, being careful not to touch. Something that feels good passes through the space between them, and they exit. Clair and Gerald alone.*

 Whole thing's not without its charms after all.

GERALD: Fuck you.

CLAIR: Be a sport.

GERALD: I never this whole time we...

CLAIR: Look. This is the hidden part of me. That thing you like. It's this.

GERALD: I don't know.

CLAIR: That's what makes it so fun. 'Cause you'll never be bored of me. Right? I wouldn't let you be.

*He looks away, shakes his head.*

 Baby. I'm sorry! I j—

GERALD: She tasted amazing.

*Beat.*

CLAIR: What?

GERALD: She tasted amazing. Did you use to taste like that?

*Beat. Gerald gets his coat and exits. Beat. Clair eats some cereal.*


## Scene 17

*The next day. Jochen and Lark in his office. She is dressed for an interview.*

JOCHEN: Will you state your name.

LARK: Sophie Berkowitz.

JOCHEN: The people close to you call you?

LARK: Sophie.

JOCHEN: No nicknames? No Pet Names?

*Beat.*

LARK: Some of my friends used to call me . . . So-so.

JOCHEN: Do you generally like to hold something back?

LARK: I didn't think of it. I wouldn't have thought it would be of interest.

JOCHEN: Why not?

LARK: It was just a kind of a private thing. It's a little embarrassing. It's stupid.

JOCHEN: Most people have nicknames.

Are most people stupid?

LARK: Yes. I think so. Right?

*Jochen watches her.*

No excuse me. No. Em.

*Jochen watches her.*

I'm not sure. I suppose it depends.

JOCHEN: Most people are stupid, of course.

LARK: Yes, good.

JOCHEN: It's good for us because it makes them easy to manipulate. Tell me about your experience manipulating people.

*Lark thinks.*

LARK: I'm good at making people trust me.

JOCHEN: An example.

*He watches her. Part of his intensity is about evaluating whether she is telling the truth, and she knows it.*

LARK: When I was very young, I used to do something for money that would have gotten me in trouble. But it would have gotten the people I did it for in more trouble. Every one of them asked me if I was going to tell. And I told them no. And I made them all believe that with absolute certainty, that I never would tell. That we could go ahead.

JOCHEN: They would have gone ahead no matter what you told them. Wouldn't they?

LARK: Maybe. I don't know. But I saw how they looked when I said it. As if they had been blessed. As if I were some kind of angel.

*Beat.*

JOCHEN: You tested very well on the course.

Do you now feel uncomfortable?

LARK: Yes. I really want you to accept me.

JOCHEN: Why?

LARK: I feel that civilization has gotten to a point where almost nobody is in actual contact with anything that matters. I mean anything that actually determines the shape of / the wor—

JOCHEN: Teachers, firefighters, clean energy experts, the Special Victims Unit.

LARK: I . . .

*Something else takes hold. Lark looks him dead in the eye.*

like to watch things change.

I like to watch

while everything

changes

and I like to

be the one

who's doing it.

*Pause. Jochen leans back. He smiles. She keeps looking at him.*

JOCHEN: You'll have to lose a little weight.

LARK: I would love that.

# Scene 18

*Weeks, months pass. Clair, Jean, and Griffon are in and out of the apartment, getting ready to leave. Clair is on the phone.*

CLAIR: I just can't do it right now. It's too dangerous. There's too much going on and . . . I keep thinking I see somebody watching us, and. I just think you've gotta find someone else.

*Pause.*

No, Tino, I'm talking about a feeling, I'm not saying someone's watching us. No one's watching us. Jesus.

Well I know, well, yeah, it bums me out. What the hell else am I gonna do? I know. I don't fucking even know what copyediting is. I'm gonna have to . . . go work in a store or something. The whole thing makes me really fucking sad.

*Jean and Griffon have left the room.*

But there's this other thing too, you know, which I haven't really told people, I'm uh—Gerald and I, we're gonna ha—hello?

*The line is dead.*

Yeah well.

*Jean returns.*

So much for my days as a druglord.

JEAN: Oh no. I'm sorry.

CLAIR: It wasn't really the right thing anyway. Compared to our gig it was pretty lame.

JEAN: But will they come for you now and "take you out"?

CLAIR: I don't think so. I mean it's just my brother and his friends.

JEAN: Where's Gerald?

CLAIR: I don't know. Out. Whatever.

Remember the day, that first Saturday there, before our first assignments?

JEAN: We went out and got lost / in Alexanderplatz—

CLAIR: In Alexanderplatz—

JEAN: We couldn't find our street, and we kept going down into the U-Bahn to look at the map—

CLAIR: Trying to make each other get one of those / hot dogs wrapped in a brr-rrrötchen!

JEAN: Hot dogs wrapped in a brrrrötchen! And even though it was Berlin,

CLAIR: Like the capital of Fucked-Up Space—

JEAN: We stood out.

CLAIR: People looked at us funny.

JEAN: We were foreign.

CLAIR: We were aliens already.

JEAN: We'll be aliens now.

*Griffon is there.*

GRIFFON: Not aliens.

Something more wonderful. And brutal.

*The three stand together, look at each other. Then Clair and Jean pick up their duffel bags and exit.*

It would grow back. And they would rip it out again.

They would devour it; no one would hear.

The beautiful is nothing else and no one is home in the world.

Some scraggly tree.

Some rat with a broken wing.

*Beat.*

I mean bat.

*Beat.*

I mean foot: broken foot.

*She leaves.*

## Scene 19

*Mauerpark, Berlin. Nighttime.*

*Lark enters. She is training a gun with a silencer on Dennis, a young German man not dissimilar to Klaus, but the 2014 version. Lark herself looks changed: leaner, tougher, more sophisticated somehow. She stays close to Dennis, who has a black eye.*

LARK: Halt. [Stop.]

> *They stop.*

> Just stay still.

DENNIS: Will Katzler come now?

LARK: Who?

DENNIS: Katzler? You work for him, or?

LARK: I don't know any Katzler. Just stay still.

DENNIS: You will shoot me?

LARK: I would rather not.

DENNIS: And he?

> *Lark doesn't answer.*

> He will shoot me, or.

LARK: He just wants to talk to you.

DENNIS: So. Good. I will talk.

> *They wait. Wind blows through the park.*

> I like your friend. The short one. She has a nice face.

> *Pause.*

> Does Katzler fuck you? Because I think he has a disease.

LARK: That's enough.

> *Jochen enters. He walks up to them.*

JOCHEN: Guten Abend. [Good evening.]

DENNIS: 'n Abend.

JOCHEN: Ruby and Marisa?

LARK: Back at the club.

JOCHEN: Hmm.

*At his signal, Lark backs away a few feet, still aiming. Jochen approaches Dennis as if to start a confidential chat. He punches Dennis in the face.*

DENNIS: Aah

LARK: Sht.

*Dennis staggers, glares at Jochen.*

DENNIS: Was wollen Sie von mir? [What do you want from me?]

JOCHEN: Das wissen Sie schon, nicht wahr? [You already know, don't you?]

*Lark has begun pointing her weapon, just slightly, towards Jochen instead...*

How's his English?

*She snaps back into position.*

LARK: Toll. [Great.]

JOCHEN: We'll speak English, ok? For our audience.

LARK: Don't mind me.

JOCHEN: But I want you to follow this closely. I want you to repeat it back to me later.

*Jochen takes out a knife and brings it up to Dennis's chest. Dennis flinches.*

Sophie?

LARK: Right here.

JOCHEN: Don't move or she'll shoot you in the back. In the kidney. You know what the kidney is?

*Dennis shakes his head no.*

Die Niere?

LARK: Want me to cuff him?

JOCHEN: It's better for him to learn not to move. —Einverstanden? [Get it?]

*Dennis nods. Drops his arms. Jochen steps up to him again with the knife.*

Please be very honest with me. Ok?

DENNIS: Ja ok.

*Jochen makes a cut in Dennis's chest.*

JOCHEN: First question. What does that feel like?

DENNIS: Er

JOCHEN: Quiet.

I'll ask you again. What does it feel like? Sophie?

LARK: Ja?

JOCHEN: Answer the question.

LARK: For him? It feels . . . painful and scary.

JOCHEN: That's not a really impressive answer. The next question:

*He grabs Dennis by the head while keeping the knife in place.*

How did they know I would find you.

LARK: I d—

JOCHEN: Come on Sophie. How could they be sure I would take you when you applied? How could they know I would want you?

LARK: Who they?

JOCHEN: Why don't you tell me that, Lark.

*Lark fires her gun at Jochen, but he shoves Dennis in front of him. Dennis falls down dead.*

LARK: Ak—

*Jochen disarms Lark and gets the knife on her.*

JOCHEN: *(Quickly, calmly)* You're going right back to those men from your childhood.

But how can we convince them to like you again?

You were so little.

What's Lucy waiting for?

*Silently, Griffon Vulture enters. Lark can see her but Jochen can't.*

LARK: I don't know any Lucy.

*Lark summons her training.*

>   The eyes they train on the world they own
>   The fingers and tongues
>   The teeth and the breath

*Griffon joins in quietly, as Jochen begins to feel the effect of their power.*

LARK & GRIFFON: The words they made, the shapes they teach
LARK: The lock on the door too high to reach
GRIFFON: But now
LARK: But now a wind comes up
LARK & GRIFFON: And where there was nothing, here am I
>   to tear the words from their bloody mouths
LARK: My revenge is transformation.

*Lark breaks Jochen's hold and shoves him back. She picks up her gun. Jean and Clair enter from different places, guns drawn. Lark aims her gun at Jochen.*

GRIFFON: Now.
JEAN: Wait!

*Jean shoots Lark. Lark falls down dead.*

*Griffon Vulture cries out, flies to Lark, looks up at Jean.*

*Jean shoots Griffon Vulture. Griffon falls.*

*Jean slams her gun into Clair's head. Clair falls, unconscious.*

*Jochen looks at Jean. She looks at him.*

*Griffon Vulture groans.*

*Jochen and Jean look down at her. They exit.*

*Slowly, Griffon Vulture gets herself up.*

*She crawls to dead Lark.*

*She sings her a lullaby.*

GRIFFON: Over the
     ke-e-e-ettle
     stands my piece of
     life
     it's my
     lord god's anchor
     it's my
     little wife

*Clair shifts, waking up.*

     Took her from her
     fa-a-ather
     when she was just
     a stalk
     great owl protect her
     wherever she walk
     Star in thy shelter
     let me be caged
     safe from the weather
     of my own rage
     Safe from the poisonous
     well in my head
     my claw in thy claw un-
     til we are dead

CLAIR: Lucy?

*Clair sits up, her face badly bruised.*

     I thought she got you in the heart.

*Griffon stares at her.*

     Sorry.

Why didn't they finish us. What's she . . . I guess she really did lose it. All those years of waiting.

GRIFFON: No.

She has been with him always.

# Scene 20

*Return, as flashback, to Scene 5 (basement office, Spring, 2003; same music; Lucy, cuffed and subdued; Jochen). The last lines of Scene 5 repeat precisely:*

JOCHEN: Guess.

LUCY: I already know.

JOCHEN: I don't think so.

> *Jochen kneels down and looks at Lucy. Then he punches her in the head until she passes out.*

> *Jean emerges from hiding. She looks down at Lucy, then up at Jochen. Pause.*

So?

JEAN: I don't know.

What do I...

> *Jochen comes closer to Jean.*

JOCHEN: What was that like?

> *Beat. Gently:*

Nice?

JEAN: It ...

Would have been nicer...

> *Beat.*

JOCHEN: Hmm?

JEAN: With Clair.

> She's the prettiest.

JOCHEN: That's true.

JEAN: It was supposed to be Clair, right? The one who gets . . . who doesn't make it.

JOCHEN: Plans change.

JEAN: But she was gonna be the one.

> *Jochen doesn't answer. She looks down at Lucy, then up at him.*

> I would do anything you want. Forever.

## Scene 21

*Jochen's Berlin office. Jochen and Jean. The present.*

JEAN: This whole time I imagined you watching.

> For ten years. Everything's been covered in a kind of film, like a skin.

> In the right light, you know, at the right angle, everything, suddenly

> *Beat.*

> aglow.

JOCHEN: Tell me.

JEAN: Last summer there was a kid who delivered the milk to the bakery. He was just out of high school. He had really terrible skin. He said he would invite me over for a beer, but he lived in his parents' garage, so could we go to my place, and he would still pay for the beer. Afterwards he s—

JOCHEN: After what?

JEAN: After I let him fuck me, he said he was surprised. He didn't expect me to just lie there. And he asked me what I meant when I—was coming and I said "I'm the one."

*Electric pause.*

JOCHEN: Good.

JEAN: I brought them to you. I thought you would like that. All three of us.

JOCHEN: What will you say to them?

JEAN: I won't have time to say anything. You know that.

JOCHEN: When you're standing over them

> looking down at them
>
> and they can't move but they still can hear you, what will you say?

*Beat.*

JEAN: I'll say: I always knew. And:

> that I watched everything you did to Lucy.
>
> Because even though she was the one, I was—
>
> you chose me for yourself.

*Jean holds her gun to his neck.*

*Her back is to the door. The sound of someone at the door, tinkering.*

JOCHEN: They're here.

JEAN: Ten years.

> *The door opens. Clair storms in, gun out, followed by Griffon Vulture, who holds a long knife.*

JOCHEN: Jean.

CLAIR: *(To Jean)* Cunt. Stay right there.

> *Griffon approaches Jean and Jochen. Jean still doesn't release him or turn away from him.*

JEAN: I would do anything.

GRIFFON: Not today, cupcake.

> *Griffon shoves her knife through Jean's back. Jean drops her gun and groans. Jochen yells: the knife has stuck him too. Jochen reaches behind Jean's back and pulls the knife out. She falls. Jochen stands with a shallow wound in his gut. He looks at Griffon.*

JOCHEN: She...

*He looks at Jean's body.*

> She knew what you felt for her, Lucy.
>
> And she watched everything I did with you. She was standing in the corner behind you.
>
> Who knows but there is someone standing in the corner now.

CLAIR: There's no one / here.

GRIFFON: That wasn't me.

JOCHEN: Oh it was you. I can see it all over you. You're covered in it.

GRIFFON: Look in my eyes.

JOCHEN: Standing in the corner. Watching.

GRIFFON: Look in my eyes now, Jochen, now,

GRIFFON & CLAIR: Now, now, now, now

*Jochen coughs up a little blood.*

GRIFFON: Who would hear you now / in your onliness

CLAIR: Who would remember you

GRIFFON: I walked lands and lands and

CLAIR & GRIFFON: Days and days, lying alone, drinking the wind alone,

> proud that nothing will bring you back,
>
> nothing will bring you back, nothing will bring you back,
>
> nothing.

*Jochen sinks to his knees.*

*Overcome by their power, he uses the knife to slit his own throat.*

*The spell ends, and suddenly he sees what he's done to himself. He clutches at his neck, gurgling. Then he falls, dead.*

*Pause.*

*Griffon Vulture gives Clair a quick kiss on the cheek.*

GRIFFON: Thank you Clair.

*Griffon Vulture leaves.*

*Clair stands, breathes, looks down at Jochen, looks down at Jean.*

*Takes it all in.*

*Then she throws up.*


## Scene 22

*Evening. A few weeks later. Clair and Gerald are in their apartment, eating cereal.*

GERALD: Feeling better?
CLAIR: Yeah, it's better today.
GERALD: Maybe that part is over.
CLAIR: Maybe.

*They eat.*

GERALD: Did you read about Ambrose?
CLAIR: No.
GERALD: I guess the people who bought his house found this whole stack of like, yeah. Pictures of little girls. So, it was true.

*Beat.*

CLAIR: Who's Ambrose again?
GERALD: Drove the late shuttle?
CLAIR: Right.
GERALD: Yeah.

*Pause. Gerald regards her.*

You know, there's stuff about me that . . . I haven't told you.
CLAIR: Oh yeah? Yeah, I'm sure.
GERALD: Like there was this time . . . the time my dad took me to Canada. I never

told you about that, right?

CLAIR: Nope.

*Beat.*

Why, did something happen?

GERALD: We were going to visit my uncle, who I'd never met. And then when we got there, it turned out that...

*Gerald eats some cereal.*

CLAIR: What? Was your uncle dead?

*Gerald smiles, shakes his head. Pause.*

You don't have to tell me.

*Clair eats some cereal.*

GERALD: I always thought, as long as there's one person who can make me feel something.

*Pause. Clair looks at him.*

You know?

*Clair looks at Gerald for a moment. Then she looks down at her cereal and eats some more. Then she stops and looks out, her spoon suspended.*

*Lights down.*


*THE END*

## My Only One (from *Grimly Handsome*)

# Griffon Vulture's Lullaby (from *Every Angel is Brutal*)

shel-ter    let me be    caged    safe from the

wea-ther    of my own    rage    Safe from the

poi-son-ous    well in my    head    My claw in

thy    claw    un — til    we    are    dead

Julia Jarcho is a playwright and director from New York City who has a company called Minor Theater. Her play *Grimly Handsome* (Incubator Arts Project 2013, JACK 2015) won a 2013 Obie Award for Best New American Play. Other plays include *The Terrifying* (Abrons Arts Center 2017), *Every Angel is Brutal* (Clubbed Thumb Summerworks 2016), *Nomads* (Incubator 2014), *Dreamless Land* (New York City Players/Abrons 2011), *American Treasure* (13P 2009), *The Highwayman* (NTUSA performance space 2004), and *Delmar*, which the visual artist Meredith James made into a movie installation (Jack Hanley Gallery 2014). She has received a Doris Duke Impact Award (2014) and a Sarah Verdone Writing Award (2016), and has been a MacDowell fellow, an LCT New Writer in Residence at Lincoln Center, an Advisory Board member at Young Playwrights Inc., and a resident playwright at the Playwrights Foundation and the Eugene O'Neill Playwrights Conference. She has a PhD in Rhetoric from UC Berkeley and teaches in the English Department at NYU. Her first critical book, *Writing and the Modern Stage: Theater Beyond Drama*, is published by Cambridge University Press.

*53rdstatepress.org*
*Antje Oegel & Karinne Keithley Syers, Coeditors*